Soul Speak

The Language of Your Body

Julia Cannon

OZARK
MOUNTAIN
PUBLISHING

For permission, serialization, condensation, adaptions, or for our catalog of other publications, write to Ozark Mountain Publishing, Inc., P.O. box 754, Huntsville, AR 72740, ATTN: Permissions Department.

Library of Congress Cataloging-in-Publication Data
Cannon, Julia, 1957-
  Soul Speak – The Language of Your Body, by Julia Cannon
Understanding the secret way your body delivers messages from your soul through aches, pains and illnesses.

1. Higher Self   2. Soul 3. Healing   4. Body Language
I. Cannon, Julia, 1957-   II. Healing   III. Metaphysics
IV. Title

Library of Congress Catalog Card Number: 2013930598

ISBN: 978-1-886940-35-2

Cover Art and Layout: www.enki3d.com
Book set in: Times New Roman, Lucida Calligraphy
Book Design: Julia Degan

Published by:

OZARK
MOUNTAIN
PUBLISHING

PO Box 754
Huntsville, AR 72740
WWW.OZARKMT.COM
Printed in the United States of America

As long as you are standing in your power, nothing is too great a load for you.

Nothing is beyond limitation – anything is possible. It is merely a matter of how much you are willing to believe.

The Higher Self

Acknowledgments

There have been so many people contributing to this book in so many ways. It was not written by my efforts alone. I had to assume a completely different role in order to get this done. I am usually the support person giving the encouragement and being the cheerleader as necessary. Now I was the one needing the support, encouragement, and cheerleading.

I am very thankful to my Higher Self for constantly reminding me how important it was to get this information "out there." It ultimately knew what would get me off my backside and get moving.

I am very grateful to my mother for her blessings, help and contribution to get this completed. Her pioneering and trail blazing work is what paved the way for my efforts. We make a great team no matter how much I resist.

Thank you, Vitaly, for being my strength when I needed a shoulder – both to cry and to lean on. I am eternally grateful. This is the meaning of partner.

Thank you, Tiffany, for being the best daughter in the world. I'm so glad you picked me to be your mother!

I am very grateful to my support system – Kristy, Nancy, Sara, Shonda, - for helping me create the space necessary to write. And to Martyn for helping me with research material!

Thank you James for your strange method of motivation. I guess it worked!

And a final thank you to all of the cheerleaders along the way – you have no idea how important it was to get your words of encouragement.

Table of Contents

Introduction

You will see throughout this book that we are much more than the sum total of flesh and blood that we present to the world. Our bodies are magnificent machines that we have decided to house ourselves in for whatever duration we choose for this experience we call our life. These machines are made to operate flawlessly with no aches, pains or illnesses and can heal themselves of any mishaps if we do not interfere. So if we are designed to never be sick, why is there so much illness and disease? Why are so many of us constantly in states of pain and discomfort? Could it be there is much more to this than meets the eye? We are just now beginning to realize our true roles in these bodies and on this planet. If you do not prescribe to the line of thinking I will be presenting here, that is all right, you do not need to fully agree with me to get the point I will be trying to make. Everyone is entitled to their own truth and understanding. I encourage you to read the information and decide for yourself if it rings true for you.

The information I will be sharing is based on the work of my mother, Dolores Cannon and her countless clients she has worked with over her 40+ year career, as well as my own intuitive insights and guidance from working alongside of her. When you understand the language of the body, each person becomes transparent. We are literally wearing our issues "on our sleeves." You will see what I mean as we proceed.

I have been guided to write this book for several years now, but found myself reluctant to do so for many reasons. One of the things that held me back was seeing all of the wonderful books already out there on this same subject. That can be quite intimidating. This is not a new concept. Louise Hay was one of the first to show that our bodies are communicating messages to us all of the time and if we understand the messages, we can gain great insight into issues in our lives. She has had a fantastic career of showing people how they can heal their lives by understanding these messages and then saying affirmations to bring balance to their situations. I was also referred to Annette Noontil who wrote, "The Body is the Barometer of the Soul," and Inna Segal's "The Secret Language of the Body." As I said, this is not a new concept. So you can understand why I was reluctant to bring yet another book on this subject to the field. My guidance persisted and continued to be very insistent.

I asked what this book would offer that the others already out there were not. I was told there is a process by which we communicate with ourselves so that we understand where we are in our development and mission on this planet. We have so much illness, dis-ease and discomfort because we are not listening to or understanding the messages our bodies are delivering. There is also a process by which we understand and act on those messages. When we fully engage in this process, we bring about our own "healing," as well as further development and understanding of who we really are. So one of the messages you will hear from me over and over again is that we must engage in the "process." This is not a resource book that you can look at to get quick answers. I do have chapters that show you how the different parts of the body have a tendency to represent the same types of information, but these are to get you to see how the process works so you can engage in it to bring about your own understanding and healing. It has been told to me that it is very important that we stop looking outside of ourselves for the answers. Stop looking for someone or something else to "fix" us. We have all of the answers inside and I will show you how this is a true statement. I will also show you how to connect to this body part to clearly hear your messages and how to interpret them.

We are all great and powerful beings. It's my mission to help us all remember that.

Another of the things that held me back is the thought that my mother has been working at this and attaining this information for so long, I felt almost guilty for getting the messages to write this book. This was a huge discovery when she found the pattern that was coming in again and again with her clients on the meanings for various ailments and discomforts. I also felt like I had not "paid my dues" to get the information in the way that I do. I realize now that everything is completely different and those thoughts come from an old energy pattern. With time running on warp speed, and us traversing several dimensions at once, it would be difficult to get me to do anything that required that amount of work and patience. I know that as she came home and told me of different scenarios her clients had and what the indications were, I found it very fascinating how you could know what was going on with a person without them telling you anything besides their aches and pains or symptoms. It took several years of prodding to get me to put these words on paper, but now I am finally accepting my place on this path. Many may wonder why one would be reluctant to do what you know you are guided to do. As you will probably see throughout this book, I can be hard headed and I don't like being told what to do (that's hard for me to admit, but it is true!). Even if it is from the highest of the highest, I will probably buck it if I feel like I'm being pushed or it isn't my idea or of my conscious choosing. See, even when you're conscious of your development, you can still be resistant.

I hope you read this book with an open mind and allow your truth to come to you. As you move through the processes involved, you will see just how great and powerful you are as a manifester, and I would like for each and every one of you to see how easy and profound it is to find your own healing.

Chapter 1

Messages

This work has been a long time in the making. When something arises from your life and living and has its roots in everything you have done, it is safe to say, it is a product of your life experiences. I was a Navy brat (a military term for a child raised in the military) and we were moving about every two years as my father was being transferred to different locations to fulfill his work obligations.

Even though we were raised Baptist and went to church most every Sunday, we were also raised to be open-minded and ask questions. I think I was always interested in things unusual and unseen. I was raised with this open way of thinking for most of my life, so it was nothing unusual for me. We were always stretching our horizons and today is no different.

I don't recall when I started receiving messages audibly. It was very gradual and subtle and started as hunches. I remember a couple of times while I was driving I would be contemplating a question or situation and would hear a shout from the backseat of my car. I remember turning around fully expecting to see someone back there. No one was there and the second time it happened, I took heed. I realized it was someone or something trying to communicate, so I tried to take action on what "it " shouted at me. I don't remember if anything came of this, but I think the important point was that I acknowledged the communication because that seemed to open something at that time.

1

I've had many people tell me they have experienced the same shouting from the backseat of the car or someplace behind them. I think it comes through as a shout at first because it is the first piercing of the veil and it is something we are not used to "hearing." "They" are constantly talking to us, but we do not listen. Once it has pierced through and we have acknowledged it, it is there as a very subtle sound or "knowing." I can assure you that most everyone hears this, but because it is so subtle, they think it is their own thoughts. You will notice that when you ask a question, you hear an answer. Most of us think that it is our self, so we pass it off as not relevant or correct. We have a hard time believing we could actually have the answers within us. I will show you in the next few chapters how you can and do have the answers. You just need to believe it.

To continue, in the beginning I was receiving very simple, mostly one word answers when I would ask a question. Being the ever vigilant person that I was, I decided I wanted to know who or what this was I was hearing. I have since found this is a very normal step in the development of these abilities. I believe this is very "human" and helps us to discern for ourselves what is what. I asked "them" or whomever I was speaking to how I would know if it was "them," or just me and my wishful thinking. Some of the things I was hearing were very nice and things I would definitely like to be real. I heard, "If it is us, we'll be just behind your right ear. And if it is you, it will be on the top left of your head." Now, this isn't the case with everyone. This was how it was set for me. This was to help me discern for myself. I think this is just healthy "human" stuff. We need to know these things to move forward.

Another phenomenon I started noticing is that after I received a message, I would get three different confirmations within a 24-hour period. These confirmations would come in the form of someone coming up to me and repeating verbatim what I had heard, or I would hear it on the radio, see it on a billboard or on television or read it in a book that just happened to open to that page. I believe this helps reinforce to us that we actually did hear what we thought we heard. This process of acknowledging and getting confirmation of the messages helps build the trust in our own guidance and continues to open the channel of communication. I no longer need the confirmation, but it still comes. I say, "Thank you," and always marvel at how it comes through.

As the veil of forgetfulness thins we are all discovering we have abilities. I see visuals (pictures in my mind's eye), hear messages, feel energy, and I know. These are just a few of the many ways to receive information. I am not special – any one can do this. I guarantee each and every one of you have abilities coming forth. If you don't think you do, it is either because you have expectations of how it is supposed to look, or you think having abilities will make you *different* or *special*. Everyone receives information in their own unique, different way. Just because someone you know is able to see visuals or "know" intuitively, for example, does not mean that is the way it will be for you. Allow yourself to develop in your own unique manner. A very popular and many times overlooked ability is the "goose bumps." You know, the bumps you get over your arms/legs/body with the associated "chills"? They are termed different names in different countries, but I think you know what I mean. When you get these "goose bumps," it means that whatever you just heard or what you just said, is TRUTH.

"They" have told me to have these abilities are our god given, natural rights. They are as natural as breathing. So if you can breathe, you can and probably *do* have abilities coming forward. Just allow them to come through. There is *nothing* to be afraid of – you are stepping into your true self.

A little over ten years ago, I was very consumed in my nursing career and running a home health agency. I had been a Registered Nurse for over twenty years and had specialized in Intensive Care and Home Health Nursing. I kept getting messages to start a healing center in Arkansas. I thought, "Why would I want to start a healing center in Arkansas?" I received this message at least four times. I started to make minor moves in that direction, but then I would abandon any efforts and retreat to my comfort zone. I had a pretty comfortable life in nursing and couldn't see how to move away from it and still be comfortable. These messages came over a period of one to two years. I even made an attempt at some kind of health center in Missouri, where I lived at the time. So you could see I was getting the messages and trying to act on them, but I was trying to do it *my* way – in a way that I was comfortable. When the last message came, I asked a different question. I asked, "How on earth would I start a healing center in Arkansas?" I guess this was the magic question because as soon as I asked it, my life turned completely upside down. It was as if the Universe was saying, "I'll show you how!" I was plucked out of this comfortable life that I had built and known so well and was thrust into my new life of uncertainty and complete new beginnings. I had lost every sliver of my previous life. All of my material possessions were gone. My career was gone. Everything I had known – all of my comforts – gone. All I had left was my family. I have read since then that this sometimes happens so you realize who you really are. You are not your possessions or career or station in life. You are stripped down to the bone and what is left, is "you."

This was my experience with the etheric or universal "two-by-four." I like to say that mine felt more like a ten-by-six. I can be pretty hard headed some times and it took more to get me to listen, I guess. I kicked and screamed and resisted the move that was being thrust upon me. Even now I find myself

4

resisting this new life as it keeps unfolding. I find this very funny since I have what seems, by many, an enviable life as I am able to live 24/7 what I believe. Most people are trying to "fit in" activities to do with their beliefs around hectic schedules of working jobs they don't like with people that don't understand them. I am around fascinating people all of the time and am able to travel to the far reaches of the world.

As I have evaluated why I still resist, I think it is because that human part of me doesn't like being told what to do. And no matter how wonderful this present life is, it is not what I had consciously chosen for myself. Aren't we silly? Give us the moon, but if it didn't come in the way we anticipated, we are not happy. I'm gradually accepting this as my life. Especially as I understand how the guidance and "two-by-fours" work.

Chapter 2

Hypnosis

The largest influence for this material is my mother, Dolores Cannon. The best way to become familiar with her vast body of work is to do a search for her on the internet. I will relay the part of her work that applies to what I am presenting here.

Dolores is a past-life regression therapist. She is a master hypnotherapist and has been doing this work for over 40 years. She is a brave and pioneering woman who is never afraid and always curious.

My father was in the Navy for 21 years and it felt like we were always relocating, as we tended to move every two years. I feel this helped shape us into being very open minded as we were exposed to so many different environments and people. We never stayed long enough in any one place to make long lasting relationships. The tendency was to make friends fast and learn how to move on and leave people behind. We were raised to be open to other ways of thinking and I believe that paved the way to what has been happening in our lives. I know it sounds cliché, but I'm often asked, "What was it like growing up with a mother like Dolores?" You have to understand, she was not always what you see today. We were a basic military family barely eking by.

My father was the original hypnotist and my mother was assisting him. This was in the 1960s when past lives and metaphysics were unknown things. They were helping a woman to lose weight with hypnosis by helping her relax when suddenly she went into a past life. This led to an incredible story of going back through five lives and to where she was created. This was quite astounding at the time and opened many avenues in their thinking. You can find this full story in Dolores' book, "Five Lives Remembered."

Over the course of time, Dolores became more and more proficient in her work with people and discovered ever more exciting and new adventures and has written seventeen books at the time of this writing (2012). She worked with UFO abductees for over twenty years and as she was working with the extraterrestrials, she started getting information that was of a higher nature than what the E.T.s were giving her and she found herself communicating with a very high source of information. This later became known to be the "source of all knowledge." She found that this source of information was also able to instantly heal the person she was working with if it was appropriate. Through the course of working with this higher power, she has been told how the body uses aches, pains and dis-eases to communicate messages to the person. This is what I will be disclosing here in this book.

I started receiving messages to write this book while I was helping Dolores teach her hypnosis method classes (Quantum Healing Hypnosis Therapy or QHHT). I would be sitting in the back of the room (usually working), and I would get the message that I was the one to put all of this information regarding the body in one location. At first I felt humbled and intimidated as this is Dolores' discovery and how would she feel if *I* were to put this together. I thought maybe we should collaborate so there was no mistaking where the information is coming from. I asked her about it and she said she fully supported me doing it, but it was my book to write as she had several other books she was working on. She has continued to get information from sessions for me to include in the numerous examples you will see in this book.

I will use the term session throughout this book. This refers to a private hypnosis session in which Dolores hypnotizes a client. Hypnosis is a deep state of relaxation in which the client is able to access information in different forms of perception. The most common way of receiving information is through visualization, but some people are only able to tell what's happening by "sensing their surroundings" or by "knowing." I want you to know this because so many people come for a session and have expectations of what they think it is *supposed* to be based on preconceived notions or things they have read in some of Dolores' books.

Through this process of hypnosis, the client is able to visualize different times/places – whatever is deemed appropriate and necessary by their higher power. Information from these different times/places can be very helpful in giving insight to your life situations now.

9

Chapter 3

Who We Really Are

In order to make sense of how you can cause this healing to take place, you must first understand who you really are. You are not just flesh and blood. You have a flesh and blood body, but it is connected to something much grander. You have probably heard the phrase, "You are not a body, you *have* a body." This is the suit of clothes you chose for this earthly experience. Now, before you get upset, realize you chose everything about your life for a reason. For things you wanted to learn. When we came here, we came with the intention of learning and experiencing - Everything! This way we can grow and develop. Without getting complicated, we have a soul that decided to come to this plane and have experiences as a human. This Earth plane has rules, like playing a game. And one of the rules to playing this game on Earth is to not *know* the rules. Essentially, play the game in the dark with a veil over your eyes. This makes the game more challenging - and fun (I guess). Back to what I said about "having a body, not being a body." We start as a soul.

This is the most challenging universe of all the universes to live in. This is the most challenging planet of all the planets in this universe to live on. In order to be allowed to step foot on this planet, you must be a master manifester. That is the only type of soul that could possibly handle what is happening on this planet (this game board). This is not by accident - this is all by design. Any "gamers" out there? You know, people who love to play games, especially the computer games. The games have different levels. On each level are all kinds of challenges that hone your abilities to maneuver around obstacles. What do you do when you complete a level? You move on to the next level, right? And that level is a little harder and more complicated with more and different challenges. And what do you do when you complete that level? You move to the next level that is again more challenging. Okay - let's say you've now completed the entire game. Wonderful, you are the master of that game!! Now what? You move to another game. Probably because you are a master at games, you will pick one that is more challenging because you want to further hone your skills. When you finish that game, you move to another more CHALLENGING game. Okay - let's say you continue on and now have completed ALL of the games out there. Now what do you do? Hmmm - CREATE a game? We, as master manifesters, wanted to have a challenging experience. If you as a master game player wanted to create a game, how would you design it? Maybe start with an environment that is very heavy and dense, making it very difficult to move around in? We are used to being light as air and flying and creating on a whim. This dense medium would be like trying to move around in the muck and mire of quicksand.

When I get a new game, the first thing I want to know is the rules. How do I play this game? Well, let's say in this game we are designing, there are no rules. Everyone does what they want (free will). And then to make it really exciting, let's make it so everyone **forgets** that: 1. this is a game; 2. who we really are; and 3. we designed this game. The veil of forgetfulness is pulled over our eyes when we enter this planet. We are the only beings in the universes that forget who we are and our connection to everything.

Only master manifesters would or could do something like that!! We are great and powerful beings who came here to have meaningful, learning, and challenging experiences. All of which will hone our abilities and skills for even greater things we wish to accomplish. Because we are here without memory of who or what we are, we created a communication system to help us along the way, to let us know if we are getting off track of where we are going or what we desire to do while here. This communication system is always working, but we don't always know how to interpret the messages. More on this in a minute.

Dolores Cannon (my mother) teaches her method of hypnosis all over the world and I am usually right there with her in the classroom to assist as needed. During one of the classes in Sydney, Australia, the class was discussing this source of all knowledge that Dolores contacts when she has the person in trance, and they are sharing all of this profound wisdom. Dolores calls this part the "Subconscious" because she didn't know what else to call it. It is not the subconscious that psychiatrists refer to which is the childish part of the mind that is used during hypnosis to work and change habits. This part Dolores has discovered has been termed by others as the Oversoul, the Higher Self, or the Universal Consciousness. In the class there was a lot of back and forth debating about who and what this is. I was in the back of the room working, as I usually am, when all of a sudden I got a visual in my mind's eye of what all of this is. I thought, "Oh, that's cool!" And then I heard a voice say, "Draw it." I said, "Oh, that's ok, I got it." And I heard, "DRAW IT!!"

If any of you have ever had "them" yell at you, you know what I'm talking about. "They" will yell if necessary. Especially to those of us that can be really hard headed!!

You may wonder what this "they" or "them" is that I refer to. This is what my drawing will show, so bear with me.

13

I proceeded to draw what I was shown, and I found I didn't understand it like I thought I did. In the drawing of it, "they" showed me to make some subtle but very important changes that made all the difference in the understanding of the principle. When the class took a break, I showed someone next to me what I had been given. While I was explaining it, someone from across the room came running over and said, "That's the answer I've been trying to get!" After the break, I proceeded to recreate the drawing for the entire class. Another interesting thing happened. Some of the students asked questions – questions that I never would have thought to ask. When they did, the drawing evolved and the answers appeared before me.

This drawing has continued to evolve as people ask questions. Questions are very important. I now see it breathing. I will be drawing it here for you, but you must understand this is a 6 dimensional drawing (I don't know what that means yet, but okay!) that I'm trying to relay on a 2 dimensional medium. I am limited and will do the best I can to get the information across.

Because of the limited nature of the medium, things will be out of proportion, but use your imagination and I think you will get it.

This is *you* sitting here reading this. This is who you *think* you are.

This is who you really are.

I call this: "Big me" and "Little me." You are huge! Only a tiny piece of who you really are comes into this physical manifestation you call your body to have this life experience. The rest of you is outside of yourself.

Here is a person in your family. Here is their "little me."

And their "big me."

Here's another person.

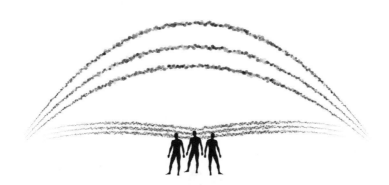

What are you seeing? What is happening here?
The "big mes" are overlapping. Like maybe they are
"connected!?" Where have you heard that before?   This is
why and how that is a truthful statement.

Way up at the top of this space is the part I see breathing now.
That's why I draw it as a wavy line.   This is "God" or
"Source."

This "big me" melds into the "Source," so what does that mean?

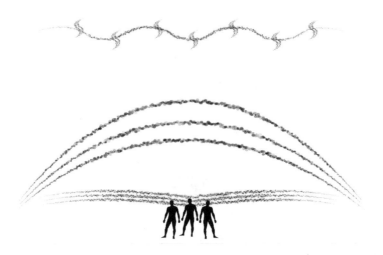

"Big me" melds with Source, so that indicates it is God. If "Big me" is who we really are, and it melds with God, then we are God. That is why and how that is a true statement.

Are there any limitations to God? Is God limited in any way? I hope you said "no," as we know this part is unlimited and can do anything. If we are God and God is unlimited and can do anything, guess what – we are unlimited! We are great and powerful beings – we just forgot. There is more to this drawing that I share when I do a lecture, but the information given here will suffice for the purpose of this book.

We came here to have wonderfully skill producing experiences. We came with the blinders of the veil on so we can have the extra challenge of not knowing why we are here and what we are doing. Dolores has asked "them" why we couldn't know our connections to other people and our plans while being here in these lives. Their answer has been, "It wouldn't be a test if you knew the answers."

Chapter 4

Translation Manual

As I mentioned in the previous chapter, we are much grander than we can ever imagine, but we have forgotten who and what we are. We came in with a plan of what we wanted to accomplish and experience, and who we wanted to meet and be involved with for various reasons. Because we forget all of this, we attempt to give ourselves messages to help steer us in the direction we wish to go. It can feel like a minefield as we go skipping along through our lives and find ourselves being hit from different directions with all kinds of life experiences. Hopefully we will take all of these experiences and grow from them.

You can consider this as a guidance system or "homing" device that is constantly giving you signals or "pings" so you know which way to go next. I think it will be very helpful to pull yourself away and look at yourself, your situation or your life in a totally objective way as I describe this guidance system. It is actually very important and much easier to get the messages delivered if you will remove yourself from the circumstances to be able to keep this objective view.

We came into these lives knowing that we would not remember who we are and what we are doing here, but we are always connected to our true selves as I illustrated in the last chapter.

Since our objective on this "gameboard" Earth is to do what we came here to do and in the process remember who we are, we have established a way to deliver messages to ourselves. We can actually just talk to this "Big Me" part, but that is hard to believe and most of us deny we have this ability. If we don't believe we have an ability, then it does not exist in our reality. So if we do not know that we can talk to and receive answers of a part of us that "is all knowing," then how are we to get our messages through?

What would you do if you are trying to talk to someone and they just can't hear you? First, you might try speaking louder and louder. Second, you might try hand signals or some other type of sign language. Next, you might try writing messages. Think of this in a similar way. You have various options to get messages to yourself. Speaking is always the first option. That is the simplest and most direct way of delivering a message as long as the message is understood. If we are not listening yet, then the next best way of delivering a message is through the mechanism we are dealing with every second of every minute of every day – our body. The body is a wonderful messenger!

The body is talking to you all of the time, so you can talk to it. It loves for you to talk to it. Within your body is an entire universe – your universe that is composed of all of the organs and tissues and cells. When you speak to it, you are the voice of God. It now knows it is recognized for what it is doing and will work in harmony with you. One of Dolores' practitioners found this to be very true when she tried an experiment with this concept. She posted this on the QHHT forum and is a wonderful example of how we can communicate with our bodies.

"Every winter I seem to come down with a bad flu or cold. My symptoms are chills, cold feet, a mild fever, and congestion with lots of drippy mucous that lasts for a minimum of three weeks. This weekend we returned from Oregon and I felt the symptoms coming on strong, so the next day I decided to see if I could prevent the flu from overtaking my body.

I said, 'Attention bacteria and viruses in my body, this is God speaking to you, and I want to let you know how much you are loved and how grateful I am for your presence to teach me how to heal myself. You have done your job, and I am now going to release you with much love and thanks and gratitude. You may now travel to the light to continue your journey with much love and much thanks.' I then imagined/saw them as tiny specks of color traveling out of my body and moving towards and exiting through a golden/white light doorway. I repeated this twice and then several times throughout the day and for the next couple of days. IT TRULY WORKED, and other than cold feet, I feel wonderful and did not develop any other symptoms!"

I'm sure there's more to this than we are even aware at this time. I've been told many times that we are only just scratching the surface. I guess once we grasp and understand this, we will be given an even larger concept about ourselves to comprehend. We must take our baby steps and begin at the beginning and proceed from there. This is not a competition to see who does it the fastest – we are here to see who does it. We come in with a plan or mission to do and experience certain things. It seems like that would be a simple accomplishment, but when you don't remember why you are here and what you planned to do, it is so easy to be distracted and get off course. The first step to making this journey less dramatic and more on track is to listen to your guidance. You set it up to assist you with any distractions or pitfalls.

Imagine you are in a maze with very tall walls that are impossible to see over. You can meander through the maze bumping into walls and coming into "dead ends" around every corner. You can search every nook and cranny looking for the way out and you will probably eventually find it. If you analyze all the ways you've already tried and by the process of elimination, find the way that works, fantastic! Unfortunately, most of us don't look at our situations in this way so are not analyzing our options to see which way will get us through. Most of us get caught up in the emotions and drama of the situations and are unable to see around the next corner and become totally consumed by the maze. We then "forget" that it even is a maze. Now, I'm not saying there is anything wrong with how long it takes to get through the maze. It is all about experiences and if that is the experience you wish to have, so be it! I just want you to be aware that there is another option available to you.

Let's suppose you now have someone on the outside of this maze able to see the entire picture with all of its dead ends and obstacles, and this person is able to give you messages to help direct you along the path to ensure you get through. How wonderful would that be? That would be like a secret weapon! Your own private guidance system to get you through! The only requirement would be that you are able to receive the messages from this other person. If you choose to not hear them, they would have to find other ways to try to get messages to you. They are not limited in any way in how they can do this. You are also not limited in ways you can "ask" for assistance. However you choose to go through your maze is entirely up to you. There is no right or wrong way to do it. It is all about experiences. Some may choose to listen to the guidance being given and accomplish all they set out to do in this life. Some may choose to not listen and roam aimlessly bumping into all kinds of walls and "dead ends." Some may choose to go in a different direction from what has been given, thinking they know best. All of these will yield different experiences, so any of them are fine. I am here to tell you that you can now consciously choose which way you would like it to be. You no longer have the excuse of saying you don't know. You now know (whether you believe it or not) that you have someone on the outside helping you. It's your choice whether to listen and abide by the guidance.

I realize the messages can be confusing. We weren't given a translation manual when we came in for the type of language that is being used. We know it on another level, but until we are told how to interpret the messages, we tend to be moving in the dark. The sign language that is used is in part with our bodies. As I said earlier, we are with this mechanism every minute of every day, so that is the best device to deliver messages through until we will hear the messages directly. Most of these messages are so constant that it becomes easy to call them a language. Once you understand how it works, you will see the beauty and simplicity of it. You will no longer be wandering aimlessly through your life wondering which way would be best for you. You are always receiving the messages, but until now, you haven't had what was needed to translate these messages. So until you discover your own, consider this book your translation manual to help navigate your way through this maze called life.

Chapter 5

Emotions

Emotions are the indicators of where we are in relation to our growth with different aspects of ourselves. If you have a highly charged reaction to something, you can be assured it is an issue you need to look at more closely. The world around us acts as a mirror to show us what we need to work on for our own personal/soul growth. The strengths and weaknesses we notice in those around us are probably the very features we have ourselves, but have not acknowledged yet. This mirroring mechanism is our way of trying to get our own attention to look at ourselves. So when you have a reaction to something someone said or did, ask, "What are you trying to show me?" "What do you want me to know?"

Look more closely to see the gem inside this reaction. It is easy to be afraid of our emotions because many times there is a big charge of energy behind them. They tend to indicate and feel like an unstoppable and uncontrollable force within us. The emotions that have the most to teach us are: anger, hate, fear, jealousy, disgust, impatience, shame, pride, pity, indignation, envy, worry, guilt. These are many times referred to as negative emotions, but I think that gives them a less constructive aspect, so I will call them the **teaching emotions**. They teach us so much about ourselves if we will only look. As I look at the above list of emotions, I feel that all of them have at their base the emotion of *fear*. So it is probably safe to say that fear is at the base of all of the teaching emotions. It has been said that fear is the strongest emotion a human has. It can be paralyzing and destructive because we are so afraid to look at it. That bears repeating – We are **afraid** to look at **fear**. Ironic, isn't it.

Fear is lack of trust: in oneself, those around us and the world at large. So maybe the lesson we are trying to teach ourselves is to trust. Trust the universe, but ultimately, trust ourselves. We have the best indicators for our messages and growth right in our core. It's just a matter of tapping in and listening and not being afraid to experience the emotion to see the message that is being delivered.

I have been told that it is very important for us to recognize fear. It has many disguises and is not always evident at first. It is used in so many ways on this plane. This is the only place fear dwells. "They" have said, "Fear is not real. Fear is an illusion. Fear is for entertainment purposes only. The only thing that is real is LOVE"

Dolores Cannon has been told many times during sessions that emotions are the main reason we incarnate into physical bodies. When we are in spirit form between lives, we have access to and are in full consciousness of all of the wonderful levels of teaching material available on the spirit planes and other dimensions. She asked why we incarnate if we are able to learn all of the information on that side. The answer was that the learning is like theory versus practical or hands on. You are able to learn much more and more quickly when you apply the emotions. The lessons are then ingrained into your being as opposed to just your memory. These emotions are only available on this plane. We can't get this kind of intense training anyplace else.

As I said at the outset of this chapter, emotions are indicators of where we are with our own growth with various issues. We can be very thankful to these emotions, as they are our guidance system through life as well as through growth. This emotional guidance system is in our solar plexus and allows us to feel the impact of our choices. We CHOOSE how we react to things. Up until now, we have been unconsciously reacting to whatever came our way. As we become more conscious beings, we are aware of our choices, their impact, and our reactions to those choices. This is a much more balanced place to function from since we can be more objective.

Please understand there is no right or wrong emotion just as there is no right or wrong way to handle an emotion. I think that is where many of us undermine and guilt ourselves into situations we'd rather not be in. We think we *should* act or feel a certain way, and when we don't, we are in need of repair. Something is wrong with us. Emotions are what make us different from every other being in the cosmos. We chose to be here now to have these experiences for our own accelerated growth. When we took on gameboard or assignment Earth, we came to learn emotions and limitations. Emotions are the main way for us to know how we are doing.

First of all, I want to tell you it's all right to *feel* the emotion you're feeling. How else are you going to know what you're trying to show yourself if you don't allow yourself the experience? I think we have been taught there is something wrong if we *feel* anything, so we must numb ourselves out of most every emotion. We are then a world of robots going through life without having any *life*. The other extreme is a world of people playing off each other's emotions and continually escalating and building on the energy of the emotions. This creates a world of drama that is constantly self-perpetuating. Either extreme is not going to help. I feel it is important to see the emotions for the wonderful tools that they are and work with them.

The next step is to acknowledge the emotion. That is what makes having emotions different from emotions having you. I think because we are afraid of what might be behind the emotion, we unconsciously either don't acknowledge it or push it down and cover it up hoping it will just go away. We have forgotten that this is one of our main ways of communicating with and guiding ourselves. By doing either of these actions, we are creating an environment for the emotion to express itself in other ways. Many times this is not a pretty sight. This is one of the things that then scares us about our emotions. This is what makes them feel uncontrollable and unstoppable.

Like anything else that is trying to teach you, you need to look at it to see what the message is. I have been asked many times how we can look at fear. It was easy for me to say, "Look at it." But when I was directly asked *how* we do that, a very interesting thing happened. I saw a little being appear before me about three and a half feet tall and it was representing the emotion of fear. It now had a form and eyes and everything so I could see it and not be afraid of it and was able to ask it questions. I could now look it in the eyes and ask it what it was trying to show me. "What are you trying to teach me?" "What do you want me to know?" One of the things I found interesting is that it was smaller than I am so that allowed me to see that it is not this big, ugly, scary thing I had been thinking it was. Once I was able to truly see it and talk to it, it dissipated into a puff of air. I guess that's what they mean by, "Staring fear in the face." Its eyes may have been scary at first, but when I actually looked at them, they just seemed sad. It's our not wanting to look at it that makes it into the big, bad, ugly monster. Once it dissipated, I could see what was behind it and what

I was trying to learn. This is now coming from a more objective place, so I can work with it constructively with the emotions of fear removed.

Chapter 6

Cancer

The mere mention of the word cancer strikes terror in a majority of people. Most people feel when they are given this diagnosis, that they have just been handed a death sentence. They must do all that they can to *fight* this disease. Because this diagnosis usually comes from a place of fear, the recipient is ready to arm themselves with every piece of ammunition available to rid themselves of this horrible attacker. It is seen as this vile and disgusting invader that must be killed at *all* costs. Many times that cost is the very body it has claimed.

I remember hearing a statement made by Mother Teresa that essentially said she would never endorse or work with a project that was fighting something as in "fighting poverty" or "fighting hunger" because whenever you are *fighting* something, you are giving it energy by focusing on it. It is a standard saying in the world of creation, "Focus on what you want, not what you don't want." If you go into something thinking you must *fight* it or *kill* it, you will actually create more of the very thing you are trying to overcome. Your thoughts are things and they create, so it would be more productive and beneficial to think about what you want as in "abundance," or "healthy relationships," or "a body in complete balance and total harmony."

Cancer is telling us of a situation that has been going on for a very long time. Cancer is one of the "last resort" messages.

31

When all other attempts have failed to deliver this message, more drastic measures must be taken to get your attention to finally look at the situation. You've probably known many people who completely change the course of their lives after being diagnosed with a terminal illness. That was probably a large part of the message – to stop and reconsider all you are doing and being. It forces people to look inward, maybe for the first time in their lives. Haven't we heard countless times that this is where all of the answers are? Since we are hard headed, sometimes this is the only way to get us to stop long enough to look. As I have said several times now, you are not the victim here. This is not something being done to you against your will. This is something you set up to tell yourself if you got off track and needed help getting back on course. So the first thing that must be done here is to look at the cancer as a message you have sent yourself and not as this attacker that has come to claim your life. You are finally aware enough to see it for what it truly is – a loving message you really need to hear.

We have found through Dolores' work that cancer is unresolved and deeply suppressed anger. Anger about something has been held in for so long, it has churned in on itself without any form of release and has now become a dis-ease that must be addressed. The part of the body in which the cancer is located will tell you what the person is angry about. For example: breast cancer may be anger at not being nurtured or not being able or allowed to nurture; lung cancer may be anger at life or at the inability to *live* their life; intestinal cancer may be anger at situations and not being able to vent or talk about them. In one of Dolores' sessions, a man presented with cancer that had moved throughout his body. When he had it removed from one location, the cancer returned in another. When Dolores asked him if he was angry at anything, he shouted, "Yes! I hate my wife! She has the children and she won't let me see them." In these types of cases, the cancer will

32

just move from place to place until you get to the source of the anger. Simply removing the cancer and having the post surgical treatments will not remedy the situation if you do not deal with the anger that is at the base of it all.

The first thing is to identify and understand what you are angry about. Then you *must* let it go. So what if you had a horrible childhood/parent/spouse, etc. Let it go! You created that situation to experience and learn things from. Look at it now with all emotions removed and see what it was teaching you. It may also have been some kind of karmic debt that was being repaid. Whatever the reason, it is now time to let it go. Once a lesson is learned or experience is experienced, it has to be let go as we move on to the next lesson or experience. They are not meant to be carried around like excess baggage that weighs us down and makes it difficult to move.

Now that you have identified the source of the anger, the best way to release the hold it has on you is to forgive. Forgive everyone involved and let them go. I know this is much easier said than done, but it is absolutely essential for the healing process. In the example above, when Dolores told this man he must forgive his ex-wife in order to be rid of the cancer, he said, "I can't forgive her, you don't know what she's done! If I forgive her, she has won." Dolores reply was, "She'll win if she kills you."

At some point you must face that this isn't about winning or losing. It's about learning and experiencing and letting go and then moving on. We get so attached to this 3d world and all of its emotional drama.

When we came into this life, we made contracts with all of the characters we would be involved with so we could have the different experiences and lessons. Some of these contracts are for karmic situations meaning you are working on some debt

33

that needs to be repaid to bring it to a balanced place. Other contracts are for various things such as to bring certain souls through as your children; or to work on a special project; or for something as simple as being in the right place at the right time to assist someone or to give them words of encouragement.

Some contracts are long-term as with our parents/ children/spouse. And some are short-term as with a "one night stand" that produces a child or a friendship. Many times the contract with a person has been completed and we stay in the situation thinking that is our obligation. There have been many QHHT sessions in which the SC has stated that the contract was over long ago and that is why the relationship is now unhealthy. It was long overdue for the persons to leave and go onto the next phases of their journeys. In many other sessions it was found there was a pattern of trying and trying through different lifetimes to balance relationships and it just wasn't working. The parties involved continued a pattern of behavior that did not rectify or resolve any of the issues they were working on.

If you feel you are at this point with someone, there is a simple method to release yourself from the contract. Dolores has given this in many of her lectures and it always has profound effects. On a mental level, you can imagine you are with this person and you can see yourself holding the contract. It is too difficult to do this face to face with the person and sometimes the person has passed and is not where you can talk to them. You can tell this person, "We tried, we really tried." See yourself tearing up the contract and saying, "I forgive you. I release you. I let you go." As you let the torn contract fall to the ground, you can say, "You go your way with love, and I go my way. We don't have to be connected any longer." You will feel a great sense of relief as the burden is removed from your heart. You must mean it when you say this for it to be effective. You will find a great sense of freedom as it will be more difficult for this person to "push your buttons."

With regards to cancer, you must release the situations/people you are angry with. The process is very simple, but not necessarily easy. As in the last paragraph, you must be at a place where you're ready to release all of the pieces and parts of this equation. You must mean what you say for it to have any effect. In order to release, you *must* forgive everyone involved. I would like to borrow a wonderful ritual from a dear friend and very gifted channel, Blair Styra from New Zealand. His formula involves making the following statement every morning as you start your day.

"I forgive all those who have hurt me in this life, in any life, in any way at all.

I ask for forgiveness of all those I have hurt in this life, in any life, in any way at all.

I forgive myself for the part I played and my transgressions in this life, in any life, in any way at all."

This is a fantastic way to take care of all of your issues from all of your lifetimes! The last statement is probably the most important – forgive yourself. That can sometimes be the most difficult step. Remember, you created this situation to experience and learn from. Get to an objective place with all emotion removed and see what you wanted to teach yourself or what you wanted to experience. At this point, you can consider it "mission accomplished" and let it go as you move on to something else. Each experience is helping you grow and develop. The next experience might be more or less challenging, but it will at least be different.

Many have said that the time they were dealing with cancer was very cleansing. Because they thought they were dying, they started releasing many things that had been bottled up inside. It was usually the first time they ever truly looked inward and analyzed their feelings about different situations. They had a catharsis of sorts because they got into the middle of it and allowed all of their emotions to come forth. Once all of this is done, the person will undoubtedly have a remission. Can you see why? They have purged themselves of all of the junk they were holding in and the body no longer has to deal with this. All of the credit is given to the medication or radiation, but the person looking at themselves and their feelings did the actual healing.

Now, I'm not here to bash the medical community (I used to be a registered nurse). Medicine has its place in helping us to address the most urgent need so we can then address the underlying issue/issues. It is very important for us to take back our power in our own healing. We are the creators of our illnesses, so we are the ones to create our health! As long as we give ourselves away to everyone and everything else to "fix," we will always be the victims. That is probably the meaning of some of these messages that are being delivered. "Take it back." "Stand on you own two feet!" "This is your body and your life – no one knows it as well as you!" "No one will be able to fix it as well as you." We must know that WE have the power to create whatever WE want, and we **can** create total and abundant health.

Sometimes this might come in the form of being led to the best practitioner to HELP us help ourselves. As I said at the beginning of this book, the point "they" most want me to convey is that you must engage in the process. I feel that means to participate. Healing is not done TO you, it is done WITH you. There are many ways to participate and I will discuss those further in Chapter 21.

There have been numerous QHHT cases in which the person came to Dolores with cancer. After going through these steps with the client, the SC then brought healing, white light in through their crown chakra and dissolved the tumor. The residue was released to be passed safely from the system. In some of the cases, the client was instructed to go on a fruit or vegetable juice fast for a specified amount of time. This was to assist the body to return to its natural, healthy state.

SECTION:

Body Parts Messages

As was mentioned before, the soul (higher self – real you) delivers messages to you via this wonderful messenger – your body. Because the Universe is simple and not complicated, you will find this part of yourself is very literal when it communicates in this manner. Parts of the body mean very specific things. Some authors have taken it to the nth degree in the interpretation, but I don't feel a need to do that. Remember, "they" told me that it is the process that is most important to teach you. If I have this broken down to that degree, you will see this as a resource book rather than a book to teach you how to engage in the process. A resource book is put on the shelf and referred to when necessary. It is something outside of yourself. "They" have told me over and over again that it is very important to engage in the process so you will go inside and bring about your own healing. You do this by understanding and partaking in the communication and internalizing the messages and getting to the root of the situation.

I will be listing the parts of the body within the different body systems and give the general and most common representations and meanings of those parts. It is not usually about a body system. It is usually about a specific body part within a system and if I were to only address the system, other issues would be overlooked. There a few systems that can deliver messages as a whole and I will refer to them when we get to those parts. Within each body part, I will give some examples of ailments that are common. You will then be able to see how literal the messaging system is and this will help you to understand your own body's messages. To help understand even further, I will give examples of actual life

39

situations or hypnosis sessions from Dolores' case files to drive the point home. Sometimes there are "exceptions to the rule" and the message does not follow the expected route, so I will share some of those as well so you can see how the mechanism works. Remember, this is not a resource book in which I tell you all of the answers. This is a book to teach you how to understand how your higher self (soul) speaks to you through your body and to guide you in how to understand the messages.

It must be understood now that the SC or Higher self communicates through the body with symptoms. The diagnosis is just a label a doctor put on this set of symptoms. It has nothing to do with the message that is being delivered. You must get to the underlying messages.

With the exception of the organs, the right and left side of your body will be another part of your message. If something is happening on the right side of your body, it indicates something that is going on *now*. This means right now in your present. The left side is indicating something from your past – in this life or in another life. As an easy example let's say your right leg is having issues. The message is probably that something right now is keeping you from moving in your new direction. If it's the left leg, it will be that something from the past (something you were told or did) is keeping you from moving forward.

Chapter 7

The Circulatory System

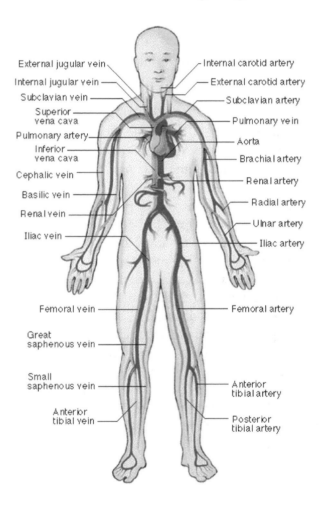

External jugular vein
Internal jugular vein
Subclavian vein
Superior vena cava
Pulmonary artery
Inferior vena cava
Cephalic vein
Basilic vein
Renal vein
Iliac vein

Internal carotid artery
External carotid artery
Subclavian artery
Pulmonary vein
Aorta
Brachial artery
Renal artery
Radial artery
Ulnar artery
Iliac artery

Femoral vein
Great saphenous vein
Small saphenous vein
Anterior tibial vein

Femoral artery
Anterior tibial artery
Posterior tibial artery

The purpose of the circulatory system is to pump and channel oxygen and nutrients to and from the body and lungs via the heart, blood and blood vessels.

The human heart is a muscular organ that provides a continuous blood circulation and is one of the most vital organs in the human body.

Blood is a specialized bodily fluid in animals that delivers necessary substances such as nutrients and oxygen to the cells and transports metabolic waste products away from those same cells.

Circulation = movement. The flow of life. Movement in one's direction; in one's flow of life. One's life is moving in one's desired direction. Any disorder of the blood is indicating a disorder of some kind with the life force.

Any blockages or problems within this system indicate issues in your life flow or direction. The part of the body where the block is may indicate where the block is in your life. For example, if it is in the legs (knees, ankles, feet), you are not physically moving in your desired direction. If it is in the arms, maybe you need to release something in order to be able to move in your desired direction. In the neck, perhaps you need to look around you for the direction you seek; maybe even behind you. In the heart and major arteries of the core, you are blocking the very love you seek. Love for yourself. And by blocking this love, you are blocking the path of your true desires. A blockage in the brain can indicate a block from your intuition. Perhaps you do not want to follow what you are "seeing" or "hearing."

Blockages within this system indicate the situation has been going on for quite some time. There have probably been many other messages along the way that have been misinterpreted or ignored. I say this because this is a central core system and the

42

body (self) sends messages via the periphery before it goes to the core. This is how the body works in general. It is always protecting the core organs or the organs that the body cannot live without. It will do whatever it can to protect the heart, brain, kidneys, etc. If something detrimental happens to any of these central organs, the body can die. The messaging system is the same way; it's following the same pattern. These are systems of last resort. The very livelihood of the person is being addressed now, so it is becoming very important for you to get the message.

You will probably see other systems being affected because this has been such an ongoing issue. These other systems will help shed more light on the situation and what you're trying to tell yourself.

Fluid buildup (water retention) – fluid is emotions – a building up of emotions – not letting them out. Not letting them flow. Allowing them to weigh you down. When the buildup is in the feet and ankles, it indicates you are not moving in your desired direction because of holding on to some emotions and not letting them out. These emotions make you inflexible in your assessment of the situation and unable to move within or around it. When the fluid backs up onto the heart, it is an even stronger message that you are not expressing your emotions. Any issues of the heart indicate a lack of love or joy in life.

Anemia – a feeling of weakness; not recognizing one's self value.

Heart attack – heart is the seat of the emotions. Problems with the love life. Feeling pressured by responsibility; wanting to escape. This can be considered an acceptable way to be released from an unhappy situation (a job for example).

Leukemia – In a demonstration for one of the QHHT classes, this disease process was explained to be an acceptable way of committing suicide; a way for the body to cease to exist.

AIDS – feeling shame and/or great guilt; dishonor; judgment. In a demonstration session in one of the QHHT classes, it was stated that the entire AIDS disease was taken on by advanced souls to raise the consciousness of the planet by teaching people about judgment. You can find more about this in the book by Dolores Cannon, "The Convoluted Universe – Book Four."

Strokes – Strokes happen from clots or lack of oxygen to the brain. It's not important to look at what or where it happened in the brain, but where and how the symptoms manifested in the body to get the specific messages.

Chapter 8

The Digestive System

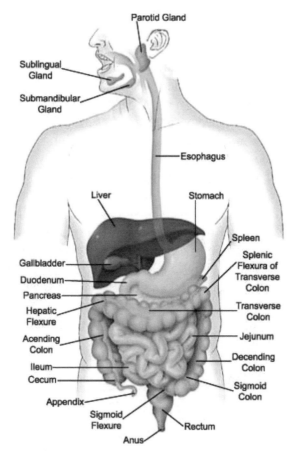

Parotid Gland
Sublingual Gland
Submandibular Gland
Esophagus
Liver
Stomach
Spleen
Splenic Flexura of Transverse Colon
Gallbladder
Duodenum
Pancreas
Hepatic Flexure
Transverse Colon
Acending Colon
Jejunum
Ileum
Decending Colon
Cecum
Sigmoid Colon
Appendix
Sigmoid Flexure
Rectum
Anus

The digestive system as a whole is used to break down the food we eat into nutrients the body can use for fuel, repair and maintenance to keep the body alive.

In this section it will be important to look at the body parts rather than at the system as a whole. The chakras play a large part in the interpretation here, so please refer back to that section if necessary.

Mouth/Throat:

Whenever the throat is being affected, it is most always the same message. This is anything to do with the mouth, teeth, jaws, and throat.

If the throat region of this system is being affected, there is something important that needs to be said. You are not speaking your truth. You need to speak up for yourself. It may be something you are very upset about and are afraid to speak your mind, but that is the very thing you need to do. That is the very thing your body is telling you *to* do. Stop holding back! Some of the reasons people hold back from saying what they would like to say are: worry about being rejected, criticised, misunderstood or ridiculed; or they feel they are not important enough to say anything. All of these are very understandable concerns and reasons to not open your mouth, but your body is telling you to open it and speak your truth! You are important and you DO have something to say!

Sore Throat – You have angry words that need to be said, but you are holding back and it is irritating the throat.

Laryngitis – You are needing to speak up for yourself in a situation. There is something you need to say. Another meaning is that you feel you have no say in the matter.

Tonsillitis – ("itis" on the end of a word indicates an inflammation) – so if something is inflamed, it is angry. In this case, your throat almost closes off as it becomes so swollen, making it difficult to swallow. What don't you want to say? What are you trying so hard to hold back? Your pride?

46

Forgive yourself for whatever part you played in the situation. It is time to put this to rest – it has gone on long enough.

Overall, the meaning is that there is a holding in of what you want to say and not speaking up for yourself.

Tooth decay – This is literally indicating something rotten in your mouth. Speaking untruths or you are not compatible with what is being said.

Thyroid problems – I actually feel the throat clinching down to hold in what it wants to say. This is a situation that has been going on for quite some time.

See how all of these indicate not speaking? It is either not speaking up for yourself or a situation or something. Something needs to be said and you're not saying it. The severity or "chronicness" of it will give you a clue as to how long this has been going on. For example, laryngitis usually has a shorter duration than hypothyroidism. According to mainstream medicine, once you have been diagnosed with hypo or hyperthyroidism, you have it for the rest of your life and must be on medication or have surgery.

Stomach:

The simplest message, when the abdominal region is affected, is that you are not "stomaching" something. Something is really against your "grain" and you don't feel you are able to say anything about it, so you hold your emotions in and it is held in your "stomach." As this is the area of digestion – it can also be seen as "digesting" your thoughts, words or actions before carrying them into motion. Just as food that is held in the stomach too long becomes rancid, so are these things that need to be carried out. They are stagnant and festering and feeding on themselves to become something very unhealthy for your life.

A good example of the stomach feeding on itself is an ulcer. This is where the question, "What's eating you?" is very appropriate. In the case of an ulcer, it is usually anger. If it is allowed to proceed with no release of the emotions, it can very well become cancer. As we have said before, cancer is caused by suppressed anger. If only the person could talk about whatever is bothering them, but they don't feel they are able.

Weight issues are pandemic in this country as well as others. We are very consumed with our body images. As I have said before, the body is directly reflecting your thoughts or attitudes and sending messages, so what are the messages regarding weight?

Many messages have been given about excess weight. Obesity or excess weight is most usually a protection in that we hide behind the extra padding to protect ourselves from being hurt. We all get hurt at different times and in different ways in our lives. The self says, "That was too painful, I will never do that again." So it goes into action to keep anything like that from ever happening again. If we make ourselves unattractive, we will not be hurt again because we will not get into a relationship or a situation in which we can be vulnerable. This is a wonderful way to hide ourselves so we are not so vulnerable to attacks or unwanted attention. This is one of the most common reasons we seek comfort in our food.

Some other reasons of excess weight can be you starved or caused others to starve in another life. The body will many times carry over residue of how it dies in another life. If you starved in another life, the body remembers that and wants to keep it from happening again, so it makes sure you are not starving. Because the soul goes from body to body, it is not aware that this is a different life and is not in danger of starvation. In this case you will want to talk to that part of you to let it know it was a different life and there is no danger of

48

starving in this life. This is very easily done with a QHHT session, if you have the ability to get one.

In another session by Dolores a person found herself as an elder of a tribe that had not passed on his teachings before he died. As he was passing from that life, he made a statement that he would never be rid of the *weight* of the responsibility of that life. Words are very powerful.

I have found Anorexia or severely underweight issues to be trying to deliver the message that you are trying to disappear. You do not want to take up any space; you do not feel worthy of taking up space. You are trying to fade away. Here again, in the first case the real you is trying to hide or be protected in some way. If you disappear, no one can see you to hurt you. When you have these issues, you are usually very aware of the hurts you are trying to protect yourself from. A QHHT session would help shed light on this if it comes from another life, but you will also be able to get answers yourself as you work through the process as will be discussed later.

The body has numerous mechanisms in place to preserve itself at all cost. One of the things the body will do is keep fat onboard to absorb toxins that can be detrimental. If you have a high level of these toxins in your body, the body will not allow you to lose the fat since that will cause those toxins to go into the blood stream at too great a rate and that could actually kill you. The body is actually keeping you alive by keeping you fat. If you want to let the weight go, you will need to work from the direction of allowing the body to rid itself of the toxins first. In these cases, you will need to seek why you chose to be toxic. What is the message? Is there a toxic, poisonous situation going on in your life that you need to rid yourself of? It may be the actual chemicals in the environment and foods or a relationship or situation that is very unhealthy for you. Only you know. The action is the same in both cases

– take care of yourself by ridding any toxic elements in your life.

Liver:

Within this system we have the liver which filters the toxins from the body to keep the body healthy. If you are having issues with the liver, you obviously have toxins in your life that you are needing to rid yourself of so you can be healthy and productive. Something is poisoning your life and usually you know exactly what it is – it is not a secret. It can be literal poisoning by chemicals or figurative poisoning by life situations. It is something you just need to rid yourself of. Your body is saying it loud and clear!

In one of Dolores' sessions, the SC was doing a body scan. Dolores will sometimes ask for it to do a body scan when there are many physical problems and see if there is anything that they should be concerned about. In the process, it will methodically go through the body, usually from head to toe, and make comments on any issues it finds. In this session, the body scan showed something wrong with the liver. "The liver. Too many preservatives."

D: In the food? (Yes) Is she eating something that's not right?
C: Cokes. Cut down. Stop if you can. Cut back on cokes ... more water. Also no prepared foods. Cook it all from scratch ... no prepared foods. Fresh vegetables ... more fresh foods. Cook. Cook.
The SC then set about to repair the liver.

In another session, the subconscious loudly shouted for the person to stop poisoning the body with Tylenol. She had been taking it in a couple of different forms for chronic pain and her liver was failing due to the "poisoning." The SC, using healing light, repaired the entire system along with the liver. It then gave the instruction to no longer put those poisons in the system.

Pancreas:

The pancreas regulates the sugar content within the system as it aids in digestion because the system must have a certain level of sugar (glucose) in the system to carry out its daily functions. Too much or too little and the body is in danger. Issues in this region indicate issues of "sweetness" in your life. Not to mean you are not eating enough sugar. It simply indicates you are not happy with your life. You do not feel the "sweetness" of life – maybe you do not feel loved or cared for. Or the "joy" of your life feels missing. You do not have enthusiasm in what you are doing. There can also be a lack of love. This is translated into the disease process known as diabetes.

Small and Large Intestines:

The intestines carry the waste products from your body after the desired nutrients have been extracted and absorbed by the system. Issues in this part of the system will indicate either not releasing the waste (constipation or blockages of the bowel) or trying too hard to get rid of waste and/or toxins (diarrhea or irritable bowel) and not holding on at all. Both of these are extreme situations and therefore, out of balance. Again, these are probably thoughts or feelings that you are holding inside and letting "fester" and not allowing to move through. Feelings and/or thoughts need to be expressed to remove the waste from your life.

Any other elimination problems would follow this same line of thought. The severity would indicate the length of time if has been going on. Anything with inflammation like collitis, would indicate anger at the base of it. Cancer goes the next step to be suppressed anger at a person or situation. You need to acknowledge the anger, find some way to express it other than on yourself and then let it go. We will discuss how to let go at the end of the book in the process for receiving the messages and healing yourself.

I'm also being reminded that it is not only about expressing the thoughts or feelings, but also taking action. How many people do you know that express constantly their thoughts or feelings about their issues, but they do not DO anything about it. They just keep repeating the same thing over and over. I use the phrase, "Playing the same tape recording." This may mean that if you are unhappy in a situation, do something to change it. You can talk and bemoan about it to anyone and everyone who will hear you, but if you don't DO something, ie. make a move in another direction or play a different recording, nothing will change and it might very well get worse, as you are not doing anything to change the situation. Many times, the message is to go in a different direction. It might be to leave this unhappy situation and move in a direction that brings you joy.

Sometimes it may create problems or disruptions in your life to make these changes, but it is much better in the long run.

Chapter 9

Endocrine System

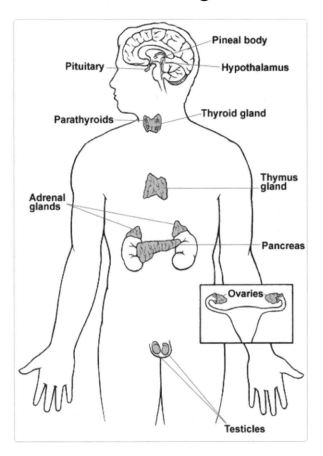

The endocrine system is a system of glands, each of which secretes a type of hormone directly into the bloodstream to regulate the body. This system is composed of the Pituitary gland, the Hypothalamus, the Pineal gland, the Thyroid, the Parathyroid and the Adrenals.

The **pituitary gland** is located at the base of the brain.The pituitary gland secretes nine hormones that regulate homeostasis.

The **hypothalamus** is a tiny part of the brain. Despite its small size, the hypothalamus plays a pivotal role in an astounding number of functional and behavioral activities that are essential for day-to-day survival of the individual person and for continuing survival of its species. Its overall role is to collect and integrate a huge variety of information from the body and to organize neural and endocrine responses that maintain homeostasis (constant balance of the internal environment).

The **pineal gland** (also called the pineal body, epiphysis cerebri, epiphysis, conarium or the "third eye") is a small endocrine gland in the brain. It produces the serotonin derivative melatonin, a hormone that affects the modulation of wake/sleep patterns and seasonal functions. Its shape resembles a tiny pine cone (hence its name), and it is located near the center of the brain, between the two hemispheres.

The **thyroid gland** or simply, the thyroid is one of the largest endocrine glands. The thyroid gland is found in the neck, below (inferior to) the thyroid cartilage (which forms the laryngeal prominence, or "Adam's apple"). The thyroid gland controls how quickly the body uses energy, makes proteins, and controls how sensitive the body is to other hormones. It participates in these processes by producing thyroid hormones, the principal ones being triiodothyronine (T_3) and thyroxine (T_4). These hormones regulate the rate of metabolism and affect the growth and rate of function of many other systems in the body.

The **parathyroid glands** are small endocrine glands in the neck that produce parathyroid hormone. Humans usually have four parathyroid glands, which are usually located on the rear surface of the thyroid gland, or, in rare cases, within the thyroid gland itself or in the chest. Parathyroid glands control the amount of calcium in the blood and within the bones.

The **adrenal glands** (also known as suprarenal glands) sit atop the kidneys. They are chiefly responsible for releasing hormones in response to stress through the synthesis of corticosteroids such as cortisol and catecholamines such as epinephrine. The adrenal glands affect kidney function through the secretion of aldosterone, a hormone involved in regulating the osmolarity of blood plasma.

The main thing this system is doing is keeping the body in balance (state of homeostasis). It does this with the secretion of the various hormones from the various glands. Rather than looking at this system as a whole, the thing to look at here is the part of the body in which the gland is located. This will give you the guidance to the message.

The glands of the neck and throat will indicate a need to speak one's truth to get into balance in one's life. There is something you are not saying that needs to be said. You must speak your truth! We have had numerous examples of people with thyroid problems (especially hypothyroid meaning low thyroid). It was found in all of the cases that the person needed to speak up or out about something. They had been staying quiet for far too long.

The adrenal glands are positioned on top of the kidneys, so you are looking at the abdominal region as well as the function of the kidneys to find your message. The kidneys release toxins from the system, so there are probably toxic thoughts, words, actions, etc. that you are holding in your "gut" that need to be released to get back into and maintain balance in your life. Please refer to the section on the kidneys for more insight into this body region.

The other glands are situated in the brain; either in the middle or at the base. As I write this, I am being told to look at those terms literally. In other words, look at what is at the "head" or at the "base" of the issue. That is where changes need to happen to gain balance.

The brain also processes a multitude of information, stimuli, thoughts, nervous impulses, etc. Overloads in information or stimuli can create a need to rest and calm the brain. The message may be to slow down and get into a quiet place by yourself so you have the space to process what is going on in your environment.

In the chapter on Chakras, the Third Eye or Brow Chakra is pertaining to this area and is indicative of issues with psychic abilities. This will be explained further in the section on the brain in the Nervous System.

In my own situation, I was having issues with what seemed to be several parts of this system. When I asked "them" and my body (I will teach this later in the book), the answer was always, "You're out of balance." The body reflects your life, so if things are "off" in your body, you need to look around you for the answers. In my case, it was and is that I spend much more time working than playing or having any personal time. It is very out of balance. As you might imagine, the life I am living currently is very demanding and time for anything personal must be planned and carved out. That is not always easy to do and work usually prevails. I can tell you first hand that the body and the person is not made for work alone, but it is very easy to get in a rut of work in which it is easier to "do" work than find time or the space to just "be." I usually feel guilty if I'm not "doing" something. I realize this is what the body is trying to tell me and I am conscious of my decisions as I work on recreating the balance of my life.

While in London recently for the December 21st , 2012 event we sponsored, I passed an herbal and acupuncture shop while taking a walk in the area of the hotel. I felt very drawn to go in. I had never had acupuncture before, but had been curious about it and wondered if there was anything there for me. I understood it had something to do with balancing energies, so thought this might be helpful. The owner and practitioner of this site was a beautifully pleasant woman from Beijing, China. We sat down across from each other for a consultation and she took me by the wrists as she kept her fingers on my pulses. I felt an immediate calm come over me – it was such a nice, peaceful feeling. She proceeded to tell me exactly what was going on with my body. She knew exactly where my neck was tight from the very recent long flight as well as some other things she couldn't have known by what I had already told her. She told me later that she wasn't sure how she did it, that maybe her chi (energy) entered my body and enabled her to see what was going on. I'm not sure what she did either, but I do know I felt very peaceful once she took my wrists. She proceeded to do a session of acupuncture as she said some of my organs were very tired. She said the balance of energy to these organs was off and the acupuncture would help realign it. I really liked her approach in that she believed the body was fully capable of taking care of itself if you will give it the space and support needed. She is not an advocate of all of these regimens to do for the body what it is capable of doing for itself. As we have said, "The body is a miraculous machine designed to heal itself if we don't interfere." The treatment was to give the organs the balance of energy and rest needed so they could heal themselves to be able to function in their optimal conditions. I found the following information on the internet regarding acupuncture in case you know as little as I do about it. As with any type of service, you need to do your homework and see who and what service resonates with you as there are many people out there not representing their craft in the highest light. This felt right to me at the time and I was definitely guided to use this woman's service. This is how you will sometimes receive your healing guidance. You will be led to a service that can help you do what is needed by the body to shift your energies to heal yourself.

Acupuncture is a method of encouraging the body to promote natural healing and to improve functioning. This is done by inserting needles and applying heat or electrical stimulation at very precise acupuncture points.

HOW DOES ACUPUNCTURE WORK?

The classical Chinese explanation is that channels of energy run in regular patterns through the body and over its surface. These energy channels, called meridians, are like rivers flowing through the body to irrigate and nourish the tissues. An obstruction in the movement of these energy rivers is like a dam that backs up in others.

The meridians can be influenced by needling the acupuncture points; the acupuncture needles unblock the obstructions at the dams, and reestablish the regular flow through the meridians. Acupuncture treatments can therefore help the body's internal organs to correct imbalances in their digestion, absorption, and energy production activities, and in the circulation of their energy through the meridians.

The modern scientific explanation is that needling the acupuncture points stimulates the nervous system to release chemicals in the muscles, spinal cord, and brain. These chemicals will either change the experience of pain, or they will trigger the release of other chemicals and hormones which influence the body's own internal regulating system.

The improved energy and biochemical balance produced by acupuncture results in stimulating the body's natural healing abilities, and in promoting physical and emotional well-being.

58

Chapter 10

The Immune System

A n immune system is a system of biological structures and processes that protects against disease. In order to function properly, an immune system must detect a wide variety of agents, from viruses to parasitic worms, and distinguish them from the organism's own healthy tissue.

Leukocytes

White blood cells, or leukocytes are cells of the immune system involved in defending the body against both infectious disease and foreign materials. They live for about 3 to 4 days in the average human body and are found throughout the body, including the blood and lymphatic system.

Tonsils

The **tonsils** are lymphoepithelial tissues located in the back of the throat.

These tissues represent the defense mechanism of first line against ingested or inhaled foreign pathogens.

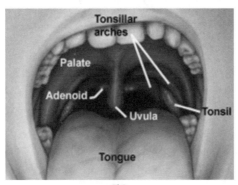

59

Adenoids

Adenoids are a mass of lymphoid tissue situated posterior to the nasal cavity, in the roof of the nasopharynx, where the nose blends into the throat.

Thymus

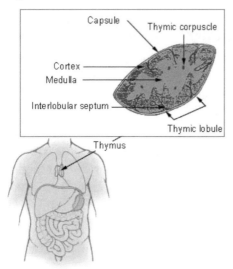

The **thymus** is a specialized organ of the immune system. The thymus produces and "educates" T-lymphocytes (T cells), which are critical cells of the adaptive immune system.

The thymus is composed of two identical lobes and is located anatomically in the anterior superior mediastinum, in front of the heart and behind the sternum.

Spleen

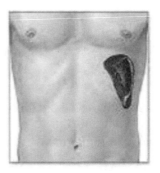

The **spleen** is located in the left upper quadrant of the abdomen and plays important roles in regard to red blood cells. It removes old red blood cells and holds a reserve of blood in case of hemorrhagic shock while also recycling iron. It can be considered analogous to a large lymph node, as its absence leads to a predisposition toward certain infections.

The immune system has one purpose and that is to protect the body from attacks of foreign elements. So quite simply, when this system is activated it would be easy to say, "Well I came in contact with someone who had a germ and I caught a cold." Remember – any and all aches/pains/symptoms is the body trying to deliver a message. It's not usually to say, "Stay away from people with germs." It is saying you are feeling like you're under attack in some way. This is not usually a full on attack, but it could be. You are feeling powerless about something. You feel you can't defend yourself against something. Something is approaching you "head on" and you don't want to deal with it. You see it as an attack, otherwise, you would take it in stride and move through or around it. You might simply be needing to take a rest (outside demands are attacking) and will not give yourself permission to take such leisure, so the body is taking care of that for you by giving you a cold, etc. and forcing you to rest.

To understand and have guidance as to the messages being delivered, it is important to look at the area the specific gland is in and how it is manifesting the symptoms.

When the **tonsils or adenoids** are being affected (throat area), you need to say something (speak your truth) in regards to the attack you are under. Another way of seeing this is: In order to be attacked, you must be a victim, so you need to look at your state of mind at the time to see if you are feeling you are a victim of a circumstance or situation. Remember, we create our situations to learn from and are never the victim of someone else's antics. If we are feeling vulnerable and a victim, then for some reason we have given our power away and are open for attack.

The **thymus** is in the chest/heart region so might indicate feeling powerless when it comes to feeling emotions for self or others. The heart is the "seat of the emotions" and is indicative of your feelings of love. This is regarding your ability to love and be loved as well as your ability to have love and joy in your life. Maybe you have felt attacked in the past where your emotions are concerned and fear opening that part of yourself. Or you are feeling attacked now with regards to your feelings of love and/or joy and are engaging your protection mechanisms.

The **spleen** is in the upper abdomen, so again, look at what is being held in and maybe seen as defending an attack. The abdominal area is where we tend to hold our emotions in and not release or express them. This can fester and cause anything in this area of the body to react.

Chapter 11

The Integumentary System

The integumentary system is the organ system that protects the body from damage, comprising the skin and its appendages (including hair and nails). The integumentary system has a variety of functions; it may serve to waterproof, cushion, and protect the deeper tissues, excrete wastes, and regulate temperature, and is the attachment site for sensory receptors to detect pain, sensation, pressure, and temperature. In most terrestrial vertebrates with significant exposure to sunlight, the integumentary system also provides for vitamin D synthesis.

Skin

The human skin is the outer covering of the body. In humans, it is the largest organ of the integumentary system. The skin has multiple layers of ectodermal tissue and guards the underlying muscles, bones, ligaments and internal organs. Though nearly all human skin is covered with hair follicles, it appears hairless.

Because it interfaces with the environment, skin plays a key role in protecting (the body) against pathogens and excessive water loss. Its other functions are insulation, temperature regulation, sensation, synthesis of vitamin D, and the protection of vitamin B folates.

Besides the skin, hair and nails being protection for the organs and systems of the body, they are also how you present yourself to the world. Depending on where a problem is will again tell what the issue is. I met someone who had a discoloration of her face and neck. During a regression session that took her to her birth in this life, she found she was not wanted by her mother because she was a girl and her mother wanted a boy. She felt "defaced" and so created this "mask" for herself.

Gashes or other types of openings of the skin can indicate a feeling of being vulnerable or lacking enough protection to outside influences.

Look at how the condition manifests exactly, as that is your message.

I have also found that some **rashes** of the skin (especially the legs) are an indication of too much energy surging through the body indicating an overload.

Many past life regressions have shown eczema (a burning red rash of the skin) to be the residue from being burned to death in another life. It may have carried over as a reminder or to caution you of the activities that led to the incidence of the burning. In other words, there may be similarities between the two lives and this is serving as a warning.

Another thing that is common on the skin is a birthmark. **Birthmarks** have been found to be residue and indicators of trauma or how you died in another life. They don't usually have any kind of health impact, but can be removed if you find the message it is giving and make the connection.

Hair (the mane) is our glory in many cases and how we distinguish ourselves from others. How we wear our hair is a great indication of how we feel about ourselves.

As I think about losing one's hair, I'm hearing – losing one's honor. In one session by Dolores the subconscious sited that the hair loss was due to a Vitamin B12 deficiency.

Nails as well are an indication of how we put ourselves forward to those around us. They are the parts we "show."

As indicated, nails on our fingers are also tools for us to use. Problems with these "tools" may indicate feelings of inadequacy or inability to "handle" a situation.

Chapter 12

The Lymphatic System

The lymphatic system is a part of the circulatory system, comprising a network of conduits called lymphatic vessels that carry a clear fluid called lymph towards the heart. After the circulatory system has processed and filtered all of the blood during a day there is roughly 3 liters of fluid that does not get reabsorbed directly back into the system. The lymphatic system is then used to get this excess fluid back into the blood. The fluid is transported through lymph vessels to lymph nodes before emptying ultimately into the right or left subclavian vein, where it mixes back with blood.

Lymphatic organs play an important part in the immune system, having a considerable overlap with the lymphoid system. Lymph nodes are found all through the body, and act as filters or traps for foreign particles. They are important in the proper functioning of the immune system. They are packed tightly with the white blood cells.

The lymphatic system is a major transportation device designed to keep the cells in a healthy and balanced environment by moving excess fluid back into the blood so it can be circulated to where it is needed and by moving any bacteria to the lymph nodes where they are then destroyed. When this system is "off," you will have swelling of the extremities (especially the feet and legs) since the excess fluid is not being moved back to the blood. Since the lymphatic system is part of the circulatory system, the message will be very similar as to what is found with that system. The blood and circulatory system indicate the flow of life and moving in your desired direction. The back up of fluid in this system can indicate stagnation in movement or "sluggish" movement in the desired direction. There is either a blockage or a resistance to the flow or movement you had planned in this life. You are "off" track or "stuck." There is a lack of commitment to the direction or flow and so it feels like a resistance. If you stop altogether, you will most likely develop aches and pains of these areas.

The purpose of the lymph nodes is to destroy bacteria that are brought to them via this system. Problems here would be similar to problems in the immune system. You are feeling powerless about something or in some area of your life. You have given your power away and are feeling vulnerable and under attack (like a victim). If these nodes are having problems, you need to look at their location for the specific message.

The legs indicate movement in your direction in life. The arms indicate what or how you embrace things or even how you embrace your life. The throat indicates not speaking out or not speaking your truth – there is something you need to say that you are not saying. The stomach/abdominal region indicates holding issues in "the gut" and not passing them on or processing them.

Chapter 13

The Musculoskeletal System

A musculoskeletal system (also known as the locomotor system) is an organ system that gives animals (including humans) the ability to move using the muscular and skeletal systems. The musculoskeletal system provides form, support, stability, and movement to the body.

It is made up of the body's bones (the skeleton), muscles, cartilage, tendons, ligaments, joints, and other connective tissue that supports and binds tissues and organs together.

The musculoskeletal system's primary functions include supporting the body, allowing motion, and protecting vital organs.

Muscles

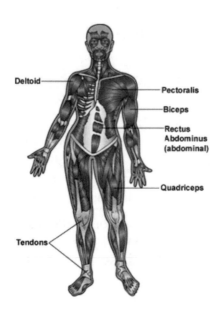

Skeleton

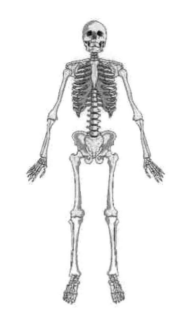

The role of the skeleton

This system of linked bones and cartilage supports the body providing a framework about which the softer tissues are built. The skeleton also protects the internal organs, for example, the rib cage protects the heart and lungs, whilst the skull protects the delicate brain. The skeleton is also important in permitting movement in different parts of the body. Bones provide anchoring points for muscles, against which they are able to pull.

This is a system that is best looked at by individual sections. The muscles and skeleton in general provide support and protection for the organs as well as movement for the body. Usually things happening within this system will be happening to individual parts such as an arm or a leg rather than the entire musculoskeletal system. For this reason, I ask you to look deeper at the situation to see what the underlying message is.

Since the muscles allow movement, the type of problem is indicative of the type of non-movement or impairment in movement. Muscle weakness or atrophy can indicate a loss of desire in that specific direction of movement.

Hips, Legs, Knees, Ankles, Feet:

Legs, Feet:
These move you from place to place. Any issues with these indicate not moving in your desired direction. Resisting movement in a different direction. It is probably something you have wanted to do for a while, but are afraid because it will mean much change and will require a stepping out of the comfort zone or a change in lifestyle. The left side indicates something from the past is holding you back. The right side is something from the present - now. "stepping out" "stepping forward" "taking the first step"

71

Hips, Knees, Ankles:
These are joints that help the legs and feet move. Joints are flexible and indicate the flexibility you have in moving in a new direction. Issues with these joints will indicate a further message of not moving in the right direction for you and will give a glimpse as to the reason. The larger the joint that is affected, the greater the inflexibility.

I have been having an issue with my right heel that could get "diagnosed" as heel spurs, but I have just received the message to see it as a "digging in your heels," as in being very stubborn. It is now going away as I am diligently writing. As I said before, I have worked through a great amount of resistance to get to this point. I tend to create resistance in moving in the guided direction. I am improving and will continue to do so as I "step" into my newfound role.

Shoulders, arms, hands:

Remember the SC is very literal. Arms and hands hold on to things and people. They embrace that which you love. The shoulders indicate how wide you can open your arms to receive and/or embrace. Arms are able to hug. Hands can act as tools. Arthritis of the hands create what look like claws or tightly closed fists. They many times look as though they are holding or clutching onto something. This indicates not wanting to let go of something or someone. Another message from closed hands in this manner is that of not being open to receive since we usually accept things that are handed to us with open hands.

Shoulder pain – Since the shoulders are the joints to move the arms, pain in this region has been shown through sessions to be that there is an imbalance in your giving and receiving. Since the arms are about receiving, accepting and embracing, when you give more than you receive or vice versa, a n imbalance is created and thus the need for a message.

Dolores has had many sessions in which the client was going to have hip or knee surgery because the joints were completely worn away. In most of the cases the message was that the person was not moving and going forward in the direction they had set out for themselves. There were things they wanted to do with their lives and they were not doing them. When I look intuitively at what is happening in these situations, I see an effort being made to move or walk in a certain direction, but the resistance/reluctance/stubbornness creates a friction or drag on the area/joint. This makes it more difficult to move which causes pain or discomfort.

In another session the following occurred:
"We moved on to her physical problems, and I had thought that her knee was related to the other life, but it wasn't. This symptom usually means the person is not going in the right direction. That they are holding back. But the SC said that it was different in Angela's case. 'Sometimes you have to slow down. She's impatient. It's stubbornness about almost everything.' They wanted her to learn how to heal it herself, instead of having surgery. I kept trying to get them to heal the knees and they kept refusing."

As soon as the message is delivered, received and appropriate action is taken, the pain/discomfort/ailment will subside.

Here is a session regarding Multiple Sclerosis:
"My client's father had developed MS at a young age. I wondered why that happened.

P: He was a very bright man and very ambitious and came from a very difficult family. And he knew what he had to do but he was afraid to do it. Mostly afraid because he didn't understand that he was to proceed and the road would come up to meet him. And so he went the way he did in the Army, and he did very well for himself. And although he accomplished a lot of terrific things, he was stagnant. He didn't fulfill what he was supposed to do. He developed the Multiple Sclerosis because he wasn't spiritually moving as fast as he should, and it caused the scaling to grow on a spiritual level. Not on a physical level, so he evolved quite a bit and he got to a point of no return as well. But that allowed his mental and spiritual aspect to really think over and touch the depths that he did to understand that things happened. And he made his choices and he owns up to that, but he's already back in this life again working through it. He's doing just fine."

Neck:

The messages from issues with the neck are again very literal. When you think about what the neck does: it holds the head in place; it turns the head from side to side. When you move the head to a different position, you change what the eyes are able to see. In this respect, the flexibility of the neck indicates the flexibility of your perspective. The restriction in the movement will be an excellent guide as to where you are being rigid in your viewpoint.

Rigid or stiff neck – You are not wanting to see from a different perspective; not being flexible in your viewpoint.

Back or spine:

Back problems – The back is the support system, so problems in this area indicate you feel you don't have support or are not supported in your endeavors. This is support from a loved one or even the universe. It can also mean you are carrying a great load.

The low back indicates that the lack of support is at the "base or root" of the issue. Because the low back holds you up, it can also indicate the same lack of support.

The mid-back associates with the solar plexis chakra, which represents your power zone, so issues here are indicative of a need to step into your power.

The upper-back/neck and shoulder tension represents carrying other people's problems or burdens. You feel as though you have the entire world on your shoulders.

Not able to "stand up for oneself." Not wanting or able to "take a stand."

Scoliosis – Being "wishy, washy" in your beliefs or viewpoint and not "standing" up for yourself. In a demonstration session in one of the QHHT classes, it was learned that the reason this person had scoliosis was because she could not or would not stand up to her mother.

Hump or rounded back – "bowing down" to pressure of others. Again, not standing tall or standing up for oneself.

Degeneration of the spine – Eroding away of one's will to stand for some thing or anything or self. Thinking of oneself as a "degenerate."

Dolores had a very interesting session with someone who had the bones of her neck degenerating to such a degree she was in constant pain and the doctor was scheduling her for surgery to fuse all of the bones in her neck.

The client was taken to another life in which she was married to a very dominating and cruel man. She truly loved another man and her husband found out about them. While he was hanging her, he was yelling at her that she was a "degenerate." It was found that this man was her ex-husband in this life. She was now in a relationship with a man who was her lover in the other life. Because she was living with him and not married, she had these same feelings of being a degenerate. The hanging while being called a degenerate created the situation of the bones of the neck eroding (or degenerating as termed by the doctor). Situations such as these in which the symptoms are being carried over from another life, can be easily remedied when the cause is found and then the body symptoms can be left in the past with the other life. It was also very important for her to not take on the attitudes of those around her from the other life.

Chapter 14

The Nervous System

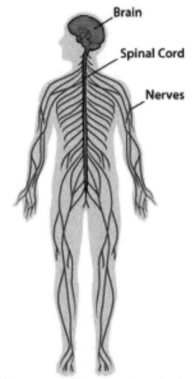

Central Nervous System (CNS)
Peripheral Nervous System (PNS)

The nervous system is an organ system containing a network of specialized cells called neurons that coordinate the actions of an animal and transmit signals between different parts of its body. The nervous system is comprised of the brain, spinal cord and nerves. It actually contains more intricate parts such as neurons, but for these examples, it is only necessary to understand the overall performance of the system and its major parts.

Brain

The human **brain** is the center of the human nervous system.

The brain monitors and regulates the body's actions and reactions. It continuously receives sensory information, and rapidly analyzes this data and then responds accordingly by controlling bodily actions and functions.

It took me quite awhile to understand what issues in the brain might mean. Dolores had not really encountered anyone with this type of issue so far, but I knew this part of the body had to be addressed. Many people have things that happen in the brain – tumors, aneurisms (bleeds), blood clots to name a few. It came to me yesterday as I was doing a meditation visualizing a column of bright white light coming down through my crown chakra and into my body. When the light came to my third eye chakra, it occurred to me that issues with this part of the body have to do with this chakra. This chakra has to do with your intuition and the development of your higher psychic abilities. We would need to look specifically at what the ailment is to determine the message. Blood clots would represent a "blockage" within the system and not allowing the flow. An aneurism or bleed within the brain causes great pressure. Could the message be great pressure around the development of these abilities or feeling a loss of control? Cancerous tumors represent suppressed anger, so a tumor in this area might mean there is a great deal of anger around the issue of the intuition. That doesn't really make sense to me as I write this, but that is what is coming through right now. Maybe there is a resentment of others and their abilities or with the self in not developing or not listening, etc.

The brain is the seat of the "third eye" chakra, which houses the pineal gland. This area is the doorway (or gateway) to higher dimensional understanding or psychic abilities. I decided to do some research on the pineal gland since I have a very limited understanding of this. The basic "physical" information I found is that it is a gland about the size of a pea in the center of the brain and produces melatonin, a hormone that affects the modulation of wake/sleep patterns and seasonal functions. I found a very interesting article by Gary Vey on a website named viewzone.com. Here is a brief excerpt explaining why it has its reputation:

*Although commonly attributed to Descartes, the idea that the pineal gland was the interfacing organ where the spirit of man gained access and animated the human body was the idea of a Greek physician named Herophilus. Three hundred years before Christ, Herophilus [**right**] was dissecting corpses and documenting what he observed. His specialties were the reproductive system and the brain.*

Prior to Herophilus, people believed the "executive office" of human consciousness was the heart. Egyptian mummies had their hearts carefully embalmed and preserved while their

brains were removed through their nasal passages and unceremoniously discarded. But Herophilus knew that the brain was the controlling center and he went on to discriminate between the various parts of the brain and assess the different behaviors associated with them.

Herophilus noticed that the small pineal structure was singular, unlike other brain features that are mirrored in the left and right hemispheres. It is the first gland to be formed in the foetus and is distinguishable at 3 weeks. It is also highly nourished. The pineal gland has been supplied with the best blood, oxygen and nutrient mix available in the human anatomy, second only to that of our kidneys (whose function is to filter the blood of impurities). Because of this unique and special anatomical configuration, Herophilus rightly concluded it had a major role in consciousness and was the gateway to our real *self.*

Later in this same article:
By 1958, Aaron Lerner discovered melatonin, a vital molecule produced in the pineal gland from another common neurotransmitter, serotonin. He also validated the fact that the production of melatonin varied, stopping during the daylight and ramping up shortly after darkness. Melatonin, it was learned, was responsible for making us relaxed and putting us to sleep.

For a while it was not known how this small gland, buried deep in the middle of the human brain, could sense light or darkness. But it was later discovered that there was a link to the pineal gland from the retinas which, oddly enough, also contained melatonin. In no time the pineal gland was being called "the third eye" and, because of its location at one of the seven chakras, it was reputed to be the center of spiritual and psychic energy.

In another article it is stated that an awakened pineal gland brings the ability to consciously astral travel, explore other dimensions, foresee the future and receive communications from loving dimensional beings. ... Thus it would appear human beings were intended to be visionary beings and be able to tap into the information in other dimensions. This dimensional perception transcends the ego and rapidly heals our sufferings, conflicts and thus karmas.

Spinal Cord

The **spinal cord** is the main pathway for information connecting the brain and peripheral nervous system. This is the message relay system. All messages being sent back and forth from the brain to the body must use this communication system. Doesn't it make sense that anything malfunctioning in this section would have to do with communication and how you send and receive your messages? I just received that this has to do with how you send and receive messages to yourself. So you can determine the degree the messages are thwarted by what is happening in the spinal cord and nerves. A complete sever might indicate a complete disconnect with yourself as you deliver the messages. The messages are either not received at all or they are received in a very distorted fashion.

Nerves

A peripheral nerve, or simply nerve, is an enclosed, cable-like bundle of peripheral axons (the long, slender projections of neurons). A **nerve** provides a common pathway for the electrochemical nerve impulses that are transmitted along each of the axons.

The **nerves and spinal cord** are a giant messaging system as they transmit messages to and from the brain and the body.

Diseases of the nerves many times have to do with too much energy coming into the body. In regular ("normal") circumstances, the energy comes into your crown chakra in the shape of a funnel. When I have looked energetically at someone who has a nervous system disorder, I have seen the energy coming in like a column that completely surrounds the person. The first time I saw this, I felt an overload of energy. I received intuitively that the person said when coming into this life, "Bring it on!" Many of us overestimate the ability of the human body to carry the energy. When we are on the other side and when we are our true selves, we are pure energy. We come into these human bodies to hold and carry energy to help others. We have high ambitions of what we wish to accomplish while here and ask for more than we can handle. Since there is the law of non-interference, nothing can be done to us or for us by our guides or higher self unless and until we ask. The result is more energy than the body can handle at this time and we have short circuits and "overloads" of the system. Situations in which these types of things were happening were diagnosed as epilepsy and Alzheimer's.

Another cause we have found for malfunctions with the nerves is that the person was holding on to so much anger that it was "eating him up." He had paralyzing symptoms. His body was not "receiving" the messages. Again, as in the previous paragraph, there is a "short circuit" of sorts on the message relay system. I found it very interesting that every attempt we made to send this person his recording of the session failed and we finally had to hand deliver it to him. Again – the messages were not being received. A very similar thing would be happening in what is diagnosed as Multiple Sclerosis and Muscular Dystrophy. The messages are not being received.

I am listing some other body parts in this system and what they are indicating with their messages. As in other sections, I will not be able to address all of the different body parts and possible ailments. Remember the purpose of this book is to get you to understand the process. Once you understand the general messages of that particular area, you will be able to deduce what your Subconscious or Higher Self is attempting to say through your body.

Head:

Headaches (severe – migraine) – Most often headaches are the residue from the way you died in another life. Some type of blow to the head. Look at when the headaches started and what was going on at the time. There might be some kind of connection to a similar time period or situation in another life.

Headaches can also be pressure or stress from situations in this life.

Dementia (extreme) (Alzheimer's) – the gradual leaving of the body's energy. The person is wanting to leave, but is doing it gradually to help loved ones adjust to the eventual death.
    There are some situations that have been diagnosed as Alzheimer's, but actually were just an overload of incoming energy. When instructions were given to turn the energy down, the symptoms were relieved and the body systems returned to normal within a six-month period. This request is done on an etheric level and can be accomplished by visualizing a dial being turned down. Sometimes you can "tap into" the other person's energy and sense what the energy is doing. Then you are able to feel the energy being lessened as the dial is being turned.

Brain tumor – deep seated anger at oneself. Angry thoughts. Resentment or anger with one's own growth or the supposed lack of psychic abilities. Dolores is wanting me to say you are not being allowed to develop your abilities, but I have an issue with that word "allowed." You may have people or situations in your life that make it difficult for you to do things, but I feel the act of allowing comes from yourself. You may feel you are not being allowed to do something, but in the world of spiritual and psychic development, how can someone keep you from doing things since this is very personal and from a place that is not physical? I can see that in some countries and cultures, there might be severe ramifications for doing such things and those can be mitigating circumstances, but for the most part, we are allowed to do our "work" in private and can keep it to ourselves if needed.

Nervous Disorders (stress, worry) - These specific disorders arise from the fear of the unknown. You feel that you must know the outcome of all events. Worry represents the lack of faith or trust in someone or something – most likely in yourself. Because it is difficult for you to allow circumstances to unfold in their own fashion along their own design, an overload of stimuli is put on the mind and body trying to anticipate or control the outcome.

The SC stated that stress can do horrible things to the body and it is really a way for the body to tell you to listen. When you listen, it gives you all of the information you need.

Depression - You are trying to withdraw or escape.

Bipolar Disorder - This is a more extreme form of depression, so this is a greater withdrawal or escape.

Chapter 15

The Reproductive System

The reproductive system or genital system is a system of organs within an organism, which work together for the purpose of reproduction.

Sex Organs

Female:

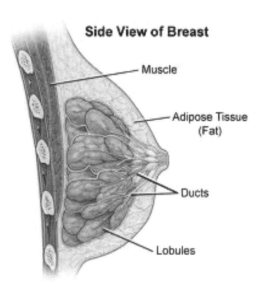

Side View of Breast

- Muscle
- Adipose Tissue (Fat)
- Ducts
- Lobules

Breast:

The primary purpose of the breasts is to nurture offspring, so issues in this area will have to do with nurturing or being nurtured. The issue is usually from the lack of being nurtured or nurturing. This is the nurturing center and will often indicate problems with parents or spouses. If you are not feeling loved or cared for, it may present in this area to get the message across to you to let go and forgive the offending person for their inability to show or give love. This can also be indicative of you inability to love or nurture.

In one of the QHHT classes it came out that one person's lactose intolerance was due to her not feeling loved and nurtured by her mother. It always amazes me as to how literal the messages can be.

Breast cancer – Anger about not being nurtured or having no one to nurture. Which breast (left or right) will tell you if it has to do with now or a situation in the past.

In one of Dolores' sessions the following information came from the SC or Higher Self regarding a growth in her client's breast:

A: She has a desire to try to rescue or save or nurture and when something happens where she's prevented from doing so, she's holding it all inside and she has to learn to let that part go. The nurturing is the best she can do with what she's given, and she can't rescue all the babies and all the puppies of the world.

D: Is that what caused all the problems in her breast when they operated?

A: Part of what Annette gave herself in this life were the many, many options and while this did not happen, this was a possibility given her propensity to react in a certain

86

way so yes, she brought into herself certain feelings of inadequacy in being able to care for others that she must release. (I asked about the drugs she was on.) Most instances they are not needed. Sometimes for example, someone may need them to, as you might say, kick start the body into a particular direction, and then they can be weaned from them. Very rarely do they ever need to have them for as long as they are given to them. (The doctors were wanting to operate.) She does not need it. It's a healthy organ. (They wanted to stop the production of estrogen.) They are fearful. They are fearful. (They thought this was causing the excessive uterine bleeding she was experiencing.) It's only a natural part of what she would be going through. We're trying to accelerate this part of her life so that we can indeed, reduce the estrogen in her body ... our way. We will do it the natural way she would normally go through. We will just do it now rather than later. What they are proposing would stop the natural production, but it would do more harm. The only benefit that would come from surgery would be whatever time she would decide to rest and take time off from work. (This is not the advisable way to get rest.) She's going to have some concerns about taking the medications. We will neutralize it, (so it could be flushed out of the system safely) but in the meantime she needs to begin to look for something that naturally will produce the same effects so that by the end of the year, she will no longer need to take this particular medication.

Body scan: (a body scan is where the SC/Higher Self energetically looks through the body like an X-Ray and is able to see how the organs and body parts look and if they need attention) Within her uterus, I believe there might be a fibroid, the right side. She just needs to let go. She's held on to perhaps having another child, and she's already filled her contract.

D: You have told us before that the fibroids represent unborn children. (Yes) But she doesn't need that there.
A: No, that's part of the bleeding.

The Subconscious then proceeded to dissolve the tumor. It explained it was all done with energy, and then it announced that they were done. "We removed the fibroid tumor from the wall of the uterus, and then we began the dissolving process. She may feel some tingling from time to time the next day or two, and perhaps a bit of bleeding, but she will be fine. Not to worry."

D: It will not come back?
A: No, it is not necessary.

(The healing of the body was complete.)

Female Reproductive System

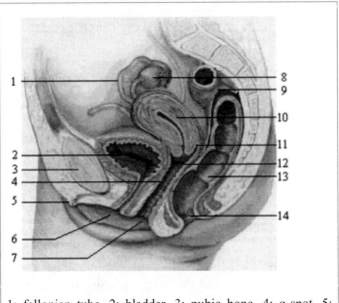

1: fallopian tube, 2: bladder, 3: pubic bone, 4: g-spot, 5: clitoris, 6: urethra, 7: vagina, 8: ovary, 9: sigmoid colon, 10: uterus, 11: fornix, 12: cervix, 13: rectum, 14: anus

The uterus or womb is a major female hormone-responsive reproductive sex organ of most mammals including humans. It is within the uterus that the fetus develops during gestation.

Uterus:
The uterus (or the reproductive organs in general) is the creativity or female power zone. This is where lives are created and protected until they are ready to be in the outside world. Any problems in this area will represent issues with your creativity and/or your personal power. They may also indicate a reluctance to accept your feminine qualities and expression. Also along this line you might be feeling guilt and/or fear in the expression of the feminine quality. You are

not feeling creative. It can also indicate you want to have children or are feeling guilty over lost pregnancies.

You will notice in the chapter on chakras that the uterus is located in the area of the sacral chakra, which governs your personal power.

Following are some explanations that have come from actual sessions done by Dolores:

A woman came in who had been having excessive bleeding from the uterus. The doctors wanted to operate. She had undergone an abortion many years earlier, and had never let it go. The subconscious (SC or Higher Self) said the body was grieving and weeping for the unborn child, which was manifesting as bleeding. The SC explained to the cells of the uterus that it was no longer necessary to bleed, or to weep, for what was lost. It filled the uterus with healing light and the voice of reason. Then it said the cells were listening to it, and the bleeding would stop and the body would return to normal. It knew now that it was loved. The SC went on to explain that her body would go through its normal cycle and then go into menopause in three years when everything could shut down anyway. The SC said it could always help the person return to balance and harmony if they are accepting. "We speak the truth."

In another session:

A woman with endometriosis came to see Dolores and the doctors wanted to do a hysterectomy. She went to a lifetime where she was a wealthy slave-owner who used and violated many women for his own pleasure. Her body was now repaying the debt with problems in the female organs.

In this case the situation is karmic. In other words, a debt is being repaid, so there will be a limit as to the amount of healing that will be allowed to happen. Usually once the client is aware of the reason/cause of a situation, they are more able to accept the situation. There are other things that can be done in these situations to bring about relief. We will discuss them in the final chapters.

Male:

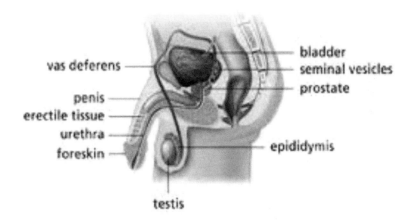

Penis

The penis is a biological feature of male animals. It is a reproductive organ that additionally serves as the urinal duct in placental mammals.

Prostate and Male Genitalia:
The male sexual/reproductive organs represent the man's masculinity. They are the male power zone. Problems in this area can indicate issues with your own sexuality and sense of personal power. Maybe you're afraid to step into who you truly are. There is a fear that you cannot handle the power/responsibility. Maybe you misused or abused power in

91

another time or lifetime. In some way, for some reason, you are not stepping into your true manhood. Maybe you're not comfortable with your role in this life. Problems in this area may also indicate you either have not had enough or have had too much sex. It can also be possible that you have taken a vow of celibacy in another life.

Another reason for problems in the prostate area is indicated in this excerpt from one of Dolores' sessions:

Mark came to see Dolores for a session. He was concerned that something was wrong with his prostate. The doctors said it was cancer. When the SC looked into the body it said that there was something there. "It's a process. As toxicity moves through the male body, it has a tendency to settle in the prostate, so he's causing and releasing. And as he continues to release, he really finds a discontinued avenue ...."

D: The doctors want to operate.
M: Yes, he has been told to have a biopsy.
D: What do you think?
M: I think his process is fine, the things he is doing to maintain health is fine.

I asked if the SC could go in and clean anything out that needed to be cleaned out, or if the body could do it naturally. "I can clean it ... can support that cleansing process."

D: As you said, it is just cleaning out the toxicity and some of it has moved in a negative way. Does that make sense?
M: It's not really a positive or negative thing. It is partially belief systems. We can sweep clean. I'm going to return it to the nothingness from which it came.
D: When he goes back to the doctor, the doctor won't find anything, will he?

M: No. Like everyone, doctor's belief systems are indoctrinations. It's always a challenge to change those.

D: That's true, but at least maybe it helps if they see something beyond their understanding.

M: It is an opportunity, a permission slip. (We both laughed.)

Chapter 16

The Respiratory System

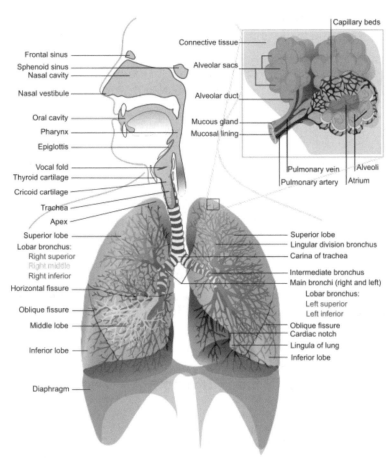

The respiratory system is the anatomical system of an organism that introduces respiratory gases to the interior and performs gas exchange. In humans and other mammals, the anatomical features of the respiratory system include airways, lungs, and the respiratory muscles.

Lungs:

The lungs are vital to the survival of the body. The respiratory system brings the necessary gases into the body to be transported by the blood to all of the cells. Without the ability to bring the air (or oxygen) into the body, the body would die. Because of how the lungs work for the body, it is easy to understand their metaphysical meaning for messages received.

Lungs represent the "breath of life." Being in the "flow of life." Problems with the lungs indicate a fear to "live." A loss of joy in one's life. There is no life in your life. You are trying to stop life. In other words, you do not want to live.

Lung cancer – anger at a life situation. Not wanting to live.

Sinus issues – Problems, especially pressure, in this area indicate pressure from someone very close to you. I have always found it to be from the person closest to you – yourself. In other words, the pressure is self-inflicted. Maybe you have deadlines in which to complete projects and you are putting a lot of pressure on yourself to get them done, this can then manifest as pressure "in your face."

Colds/Flu – you are being indecisive about something and you need to make a decision. You are trying to delay the action. This is also a way to force you to rest.

Asthma – (constricts the flow of air) – being restricted; feeling smothered by individuals or situations; not being allowed to "breathe." Many times you will find the cause or link to asthma in a past life. It will usually be from the way you died in another life from strangulation, drowning or other type of asphyxiation and carried over the residue from that death. Once the association is found, the asthma will disappear.

In one of Dolores Cannon's sessions the subconscious (higher self) had this to say about asthma:

P: That's a label that doesn't merit accurate description. A lot of it is related to the choices to feel stagnant, or restricted, in giving love. Because how he understands *doing* is in a state of *being* where he is able to share his gifts of love with others. And the social dynamic of giving love initially upon meeting someone, and that that's not appropriate to do, is nonsense. And he knows this. Give everything you have to give right now.
D: He believed the asthma to be real.
P: The word doesn't have any usefulness anymore. This will be his feedback though. He also occasionally developed pneumonia. That was the time when he was withholding the most love, and feeling the most stuck, and the least free points of his life.

The Sub. then went about healing the body.

P: It needs to be aligned; it's just out of alignment. Creating the sounds and the symbol codes that will resonate to pull everything together as it should work. As long as he follows through. That's a big lesson he has yet to fully learn in this life. To continue doing what he said he will do – to follow through. He understands that term very well. (A comment on food) The most effective thing he can remove from his diet is cheese. And he really likes cheese, so he's not going to want to hear that. It retains too much radiation for his body. Milk products retain an enormous amount of radiation. (That was a surprise!) Cold pasteurization is not good.

97

"They" have said repeatedly that *live* foods are the best foods to consume. This means fresh fruits and vegetables.

Chapter 17

The Sensory System

Sight - Eyes

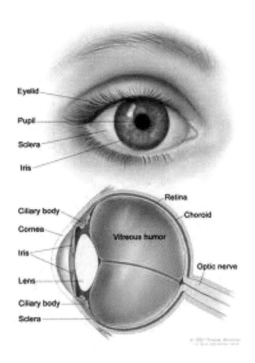

The human eye is an organ which reacts to light for several purposes. As a conscious sense organ, the eye allows vision. Rod and cone cells in the retina allow conscious light perception and vision including color differentiation and the perception of depth. The human eye can distinguish about 10 million colors.

The eyes are used for "seeing." This can be seeing in this dimension or in others or your situation in general. The word "seeing" is used many times to indicate "understanding." Because of this, often the meaning of eye disorders will be that you are not understanding something (either by choice or confusion). Most of the times, the message will be some variation on the ability to see what is going on.

Blurred vision – There is fear or denial and you do not want to see your situation clearly. You are afraid of what you will see if it is clear. You want to "soften" the reality of what you are seeing.

Near-sighted (the ablility to see clearly up close, but not at a distance) – There is a fear of your future; a fear of what is coming "down the road." Many times, this is a caution because unpleasant things have happened in the present, so you guard yourself from possible "hurts" in the future. On a subconscious level, we know great changes are coming and many are afraid to see them. Again, we tend to fear what we don't know and we tend to brace ourselves for change.

Far-sighted (the ablility to see clearly at a distance, but not up close) – What don't you want to see in your life right now. You're afraid to see your situation clearly. You think things will be better later and you don't really want to look at the situation now. There is an unwillingness or fear to "see" things as they really are.

Double vision – another way of not focusing on what is right in front of you. You wish to distort the reality so it is easier to deal with.

Cataracts – There is a gradual blurring or fading of what you are seeing. This indicates a stronger or more insistent message of something or a situation that needs to be seen. This has been happening for a while and you have not understood the message.

Glaucoma – I'm feeling this is a denial of what is being seen. Not wanting to admit or deal with what is right in front of you; a total fogging over of the reality of the situation.

Hearing

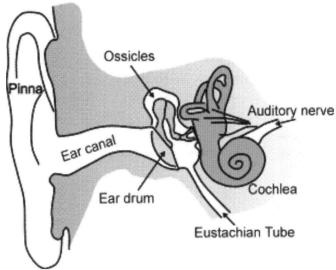

Ears:

The ears represent hearing. The type of issue you are having with the ears will give an indication of the problem you are having with hearing. It can be listening to internal guidance or to others. We can be a very stubborn people. Our guides are constantly trying to talk to us. Many times when I look etherically at someone using my third eye vision, I see guides and angels right up to one of the ears trying very hard to be heard. I've been told many times that we need to listen with different ears and see with different eyes. This means we need to listen and see from our internal sensors that have nothing to do with their physical counterparts. These counterparts are used to deliver the messages. They make great symbols for the messages.

Difficulty Hearing or Hearing Loss – What don't you want to hear? This can be now or in the past depending on which side it is (left – past; right – now). It can also be resistance to hearing your inner guidance. Other meanings can be that you do not want to listen to others or you don't like to be told what to do. (I'm guilty of that one.)

Itching or Burning sensation of ears – this is an irritant to the ears and can be negative self-talk or not wanting to hear something (maybe something is very irritating) in the past or now depending on which ear it is. A conflict in what you are hearing. Maybe what someone is telling you is not in agreement with what you know or are seeing.

Ringing in the ears (tinnitus) – a frequency adjustment - a calling to raise your frequency. You can either ask the energy to be turned down or you must raise your own vibration to tune in. You raise your vibrations by thinking light, high vibration thoughts. "I am God" or "Light, light" or "Up, up, up" are good ones to lighten your energy. Conversely, you can ask the energy to be turned down by seeing an etheric dial and see yourself turning it down until the ringing stops. I decided to experiment with this after I learned it was a frequency adjustment. The next time I had ringing in my ear (it's usually my left ear, but not always), I decided to think uplifting thoughts like "I am God" or "up, up, up." The ringing subsided immediately. I used to think maybe I would hear something within the ringing, but that hasn't happened yet. It just goes away and I guess I have raised my frequency a little.

Smell - Nose

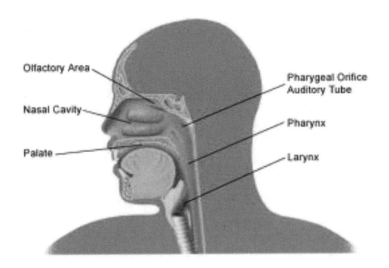

Anything with the nose indicates something right in front of you – "plain as the nose on your face" – something so close – it can't get any closer to be seen by you. "It's in your face."

Another meaning can be "sticking your nose where it doesn't belong" – getting into other's business. It's something very close to you, that's why it is right in your face.

An example Dolores has had with a session was someone who, in another life, created smelly potions of herbs and plants. In this current life when she was young and in ill health, her grandmother created a poultice of herbs to aid in her healing.

The smell apparently brought back memories of the horrible smells from this other life. Because these unpleasant smells awakened memories, her sense of smell completely shut down. Once the information was found as to where this came from, the sensitivity to the smells was left with the other life so her sense of smell could be returned to this current life.

Another example of a message being delivered using the nose:

I saw an old friend one day and he had a bandage on his nose. I asked what happened and he said he had some skin cancer removed. This person had been very tired of his life in his current profession. He knew he needed to make some changes and at this time had not made them yet. I received a message that the situation was "in his face" so he would have to look at it and make some changes and that the solution was "as clear as the nose on his face." When I discussed this further with him, he said he did have a solution, but wouldn't be able to put it into action for a few months. I'm sure once he started acting on this new plan, his conditions cleared.

Once the message is received, understood and acted upon, there is no longer the need for the message.

Chapter 18

The Urinary System

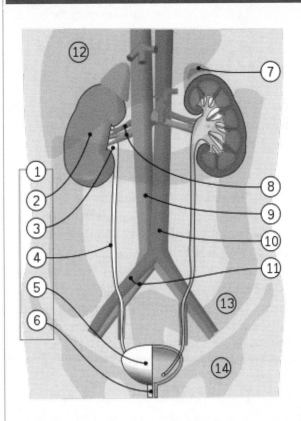

1. *Human urinary system:* 2. Kidney, 3. Renal pelvis, 4. Ureter, **5. Urinary bladder**, 6. Urethra. (Left side with frontal section)   7. Adrenal gland
Vessels: 8. Renal artery and vein, 9. Inferior vena cava, 10. Abdominal aorta, 11. Common iliac artery and vein
12. Liver, 13. Large intestine, 14. Pelvis

The **kidneys** are essential in the urinary system and also serve homeostatic functions such as the regulation of electrolytes, maintenance of acid-base balance, and regulation of blood pressure (via maintaining salt and water balance). They serve the body as a natural filter of the blood, and remove wastes which are diverted to the urinary bladder. In producing urine, the kidneys excrete wastes such as urea and ammonium; the kidneys also are responsible for the reabsorption of water, glucose, and amino acids. The kidneys also produce hormones including calcitriol, erythropoietin, and the enzyme renin.

Each kidney excretes urine into a ureter, itself a paired structure that empties into the urinary bladder.

The urinary bladder is the organ that collects urine excreted by the kidneys before disposal by urination.

The urinary system is primarily used to eliminate waste products from the body as well as keep the body in balance. If waste products were left in the body and allowed to accumulate, it would be like letting garbage pile up in your home. It would smell as it began and continued to decay, which would create toxic gases that could be harmful to your very existence. The kidneys filter all of the blood flowing through the body, so I see this as a form of discernment. The kidneys keep the body in balance while discernment can help keep your life in balance. They are used to "filter" out things and situations that are not right for you.

If something is wrong in this system (ie. Kidneys, bladder, ureters, etc.), it can be indicating an issue with letting go of a toxic situation or waste in your life. Because this system or these organs deal with waste products and toxins like the colon and the liver, there will be similar meanings. If the problem you are having with any of these organs has to do with

106

frequency of releasing (in other words, frequent urination or diarrhea with the colon), then the issue has to with wanting to get something out of your life. You really want to release this toxic situation. You know it's not good or healthy for you and you are trying to get it out. The opposite is true if you are having symptoms of inability to "go," then the message is that you are trying to hold on to a toxic or unhealthy situation. If there is an infection, that is again from not releasing what needs to be shed and it is showing you that this is not compatible with you and your life. The messages are loud and clear that the situation you are holding on to and not wanting to release is very unhealthy for you.

Kidney/Liver Disorders – Firstly, rid the body of deadly toxins/poisons. Secondly, what are you trying to get out of your life? What is poisoning your life?

Chapter 19

Chakras

I was receiving a follow-up treatment to an atlas profilax procedure while on one of my trips to England. An AtlasPROfilax® is a strategic and non-chiropractic massage which is applied to the short musculature of the neck of the soft-tissue that holds the Atlas in place. Its purpose is to safely and permanently return the Atlas bone to its correct position in only one application. Old patterns clear and the entire system begins to function to its fullest potential. The revolutionary method was developed by R. C. Schumperli between 1993 and 1996. This is not for everyone. It resonated with me and I felt drawn to get the procedure. During this procedure, I was found to have some residual issues in the mid-back/spine area. I am always looking for the underlying message of everything that happens, so naturally I started asking "myself" what that area represented. This is an area of the back that had been eluding me. I got messages for the low and upper backs, but so far, nothing for the mid-back. As I asked what this could be, I received the message, "Remember the chakras." So I started thinking, what chakra is around here? Then I realized the solar plexus chakra is directly across from this section of the back. I was then reminded that this chakra is about one's personal power. Then as I thought it out, I was told this is a matter of stepping into my personal power and my resistance to it. That made so much sense! I was then told that I needed to incorporate the chakras into this book as they play a very important role in understanding the messages being delivered by the body.

I'm not very knowledgeable about chakras. I know the basic seven, what color they are and roughly what each one is about. So I had to do some research if I was going to write anything intelligent about the subject. I looked at everything I could find on the Internet so I could shed some light on this and figure how chakras enter into this way of thinking and healing. I know it is important that the chakras are in balance and spinning, but what does that really mean?

I was astounded by what I found. It amazes me how intertwined all of this is. I found some sites that broke down the information for each chakra in such a way as to show what body parts they affect and what physical dysfunctions you might see when they are out of balance. I will show you in a minute what I mean, but right now I will give some basic, introductory information on what a chakra is and what it does.

The study of chakras is very old. They are first mentioned in the Vedas, ancient Hindu texts of knowledge. The subject can be very detailed and complicated, but we do not need that much information in order to understand their roles here. There are volumes of information as well as countless classes being taught on the subject if you would like to delve into this further.

As defined in About.com – Holistic Healing by Phylameana lila Desy:

Chakras are our energy centers. They are the openings for life energy to flow into and out of our aura. Their function is to vitalize the physical body and to bring about the development of our self-consciousness. They are associated with our physical, mental and emotional interactions. There are seven major chakras. The first (root) actually hangs outside of your body. It is located between your thighs, about half way between your knees and your physical body. The seventh chakra (crown) is located on the top of your head. The

110

remaining chakras (sacral, solar plexus, heart, throat, and third eye), are aligned in sequence along your spine, neck and skull. The chakras look similar to funnels with petal-like openings. Chakras are invisible to the human eye, but they can be perceived intuitively by trained energyworkers.

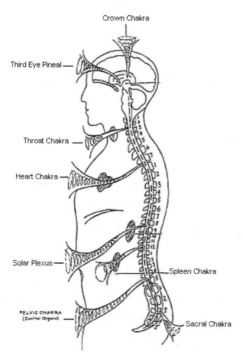

The aura is the energy field around each individual. We all have these energy fields and these chakras are the different points at which the energy flows in and out. When you are ill or have low energy, it is certain that one or more your chakras is not functioning at optimal capacity. It is not the illness that caused this, but rather the low flow of energy for whatever reason that is causing the illness. There are many things that can cause a reduction in the energy flow and I will discuss those a little later in this chapter.

Heather Stuart has this to say in her book, "How to Hear Source in the Supermarket."

If your chakras are out of alignment or clogged-up, then there are usually some physical symptoms which accompany this imbalance. These imbalances may develop temporarily or they may become chronic. They may come from current situations, family, culture, past lives or other old baggage that you're still hanging on to. Your chakra may be deficient or over-active. Think of a depressed person who has slumped shoulders–their heart chakra may be under-active or closed. Or think of a person who talks too much and never listens–their throat chakra may be in excess or over-active.

Crystalinks.com (metaphysics and science website) has this to say about chakras.

Chakra means wheel in Sanskrit. Consciousness and energy move from one frequency to another in spiraling fashion. The body has energy centers that look like spinning wheels and are called Chakras. They allow energy to flow from one part of the body to another. As with all things in our reality, they are linked to sound, light and color. To heal, is to bring the chakras into alignment and balance and then understand the nature of creation and your purpose in it.

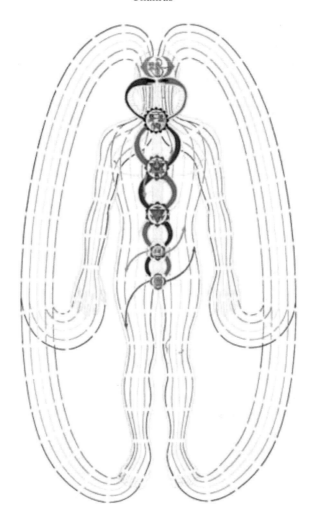

As you can see, it is very important to engage in the process. Sometimes it's like being a detective, figuring out what each thing is trying to tell you.

Per reiki-for-holistic-health.com:

The chakras are constantly rotating and vibrating. The activities in them influence our: Body shape, Glandular processes, Chronic physical ailments, Thoughts, and Behavior. When one (or more) of the chakras is blocked and the energy

113

does not flow harmoniously through them, or it is wide open, it will result in imbalance that is manifested in all areas of life. Each chakra is expressed on the physical body in one of the endocrine glands that regulate physical and emotional processes in the body. The imbalance in the chakra will also be expressed in the endocrine gland linked to it.

This is the part I found so fascinating. Each of the chakras is associated with one of the endocrine glands which is associated with different body parts and physical functions. We knew the parts of the bodies were giving messages, but now we can link the chakras and endocrine system to the same messages. This validates the entire messaging system!

There are seven main chakras that are located along the central line of the body, from the base of the spine to the top of the head.

❖ The First or Root Chakra (red)

This chakra is located at the base of the spine and it has as its central issue: survival, stability, acceptance, self-preservation, deep-rootedness, perception, grounding, fear and safety. The root chakra is powerfully related to our contact with the Earth, providing us with the ability to be grounded into the earth plane. This is also the center of manifestation. When you are trying to make things happen in the material world, business or material possessions, the energy to succeed will come from this first chakra. The body parts for this root chakra include the hips, legs, lower back, and sexual organs (men). The endocrine glands associated with it are the Sexual and Adrenal glands.

The physical dysfunctions associated with the imbalance of this chakra are: frequent illness, disorders of the bowel, large intestine, problems with legs, feet, base of spine (chronic low back pain, sciatica), eating disorders, fearfulness, being anxious, insecure and frustrated. Problems like obesity, anorexia nervosa, and knee troubles can occur.

The possible messages from this chakra could be: base of the spine= base of the issue; stability. Legs and feet= deep rootedness; fear to move; inability to ground. Large intestine problems/eating disorders= acceptance; survival; holding on or eliminating something from the life.

❖ The Second or Sacral Chakra (orange)

This chakra is located two inches below the navel and has as its central issue: sexuality, emotions, financial, creativity, codes of honor and ethics. It governs people's sense of self-worth, their confidence in their own creativity, and their ability to relate to others in an open and friendly way. The body parts for this chakra include the sexual organs (women), kidneys, bladder, and large intestine. The endocrine gland associated with it is the Pancreas.

The physical dysfunctions associated with the imbalance or blockage of this chakra are: sexual dysfunctions; dysfunctions of the reproductive organs, spleen, urinary system; loss of appetite for food, sex, life; chronic lower back pain, sciatica; feeling emotionally explosive or manipulative; kidney weakness; constipation; and muscle spasms.

The abdomen is where we tend to hold our emotions – they become blocked and create intestinal problems. The kidneys, intestines, bladder are all used to

115

eliminate waste and toxins from the body = dysfunctions here indicate a desire to be rid of a toxic situation or some type of toxins from one's life.

Constipation is indicative of holding on to some situation and not being able to let go.

❖ The Third or Solar Plexus Chakra (yellow)

This chakra is located two inches below the breastbone in the center behind the stomach. The third chakra is the center of personal power, the place of ego, of passions, impulses, anger and strength. The body parts for this chakra include the stomach, liver, gall bladder, pancreas, and small intestine. The endocrine glands associated with it are the Pancreas and the Adrenal.

When this chakra is out of balance or blocked you may lack confidence, be confused, worry about what others think, feel others are controlling your life, and may be depressed. Physical problems may include digestive difficulties, colon and intestinal problems, anorexia or bulimia, pancreatitis, liver problems, diabetes, nervous exhaustion, and food allergies.

Again, since this is in the abdominal area where we carry and hold emotions, the messages might be about releasing the emotions held in this area. Also, to step into your personal power and not give it away. Mid-back pain could represent a conflict within your own perception of your power.

❖ The Fourth or Heart Chakra (green)

This chakra is located behind the breastbone in front and on the spine between the shoulder blades in back. This is the center or seat of the emotions. It is the

116

center for love, compassion and spirituality. This center directs one's ability to love themselves and others, to give and receive love. This is also the chakra connecting body and mind with spirit. The body parts for this chakra include the heart, lungs, circulatory system, shoulders, and upper back. The endocrine gland associated with it is the Thymus gland.

When this chakra is out of balance or blocked, you may feel sorry for yourself, paranoid, indecisive, afraid of letting go, afraid of getting hurt, or unworthy of love. Some of the physical dysfunctions associated with this imbalanced situation are: disorders of the heart, lungs, thymus, breast, arms, asthma, allergy, circulation problems, immune system deficiency, and tension between the shoulder blades.

The heart is the seat of the emotions and where we feel love. Problems with the heart indicate a lack of love in one's life or lack of love for life. The lungs are in this region and indicate a fear to live life. The lungs represent the breath of life, so problems in this area can indicate a restriction in living. The type of problem will give an indication of what the message is. There is a lot of fear when the lungs are involved.

❖ The Fifth or Throat Chakra (blue)

This fifth chakra is located in the V of the collarbone at the lower neck and is the center of communication, sound and expression of creativity via thought, speech, and writing. The body parts for the fifth chakra are the throat, neck, teeth, ears, and thyroid gland. The endocrine glands associated with it are the Thyroid and Parathyroid.

When this chakra is blocked or out of balance, you may want to hold back, feel timid, be quiet, feel weak, or can't express your thoughts. Physical illnesses or ailments include: thyroid problems, ear infections and problems, raspy throat, chronic sore throat, mouth ulcers, gum difficulties, scoliosis, laryngitis, swollen glands, headaches, pain in the neck and shoulders.

Anything in this area indicates a need to speak out or tell one's truth. There is something you need to say, but are afraid to.

❖ The Sixth or Third Eye Chakra (dark blue)

The sixth chakra is located above the physical eyes on the center of the forehead. This is the center for physical ability, higher intuition, the energies of spirit and light. Through the power of the sixth chakra, you can receive guidance, channel, and tune into your Higher Self. The body parts of this chakra include: the eyes, face, brain, lymphatic and endocrine system. The endocrine glands associated with it are the Pituitary and the Pineal glands.

When the sixth chakra is blocked or out of balance you may feel non-assertive, afraid of success, or go the opposite way and be egotistical. Physical symptoms or dysfunctions include: headaches; eye and ear disease; nose and sinus problems; brain tumor; neurological disturbances; seizures; learning difficulties.

This covers the eyes and ears which indicate not wanting to see or hear something. Also the nose, sinus, and brain are covered here indicating something very close to you (maybe yourself), is applying pressure or deadlines. The brain can represent anger or resentment at others' spiritual and intuitive development, or your lack or delay in growth or what you "expected" to happen. Please remember, this is not a race in spiritual development. We are all developing at our own paces and with our own gifts and abilities.

❖ The Seventh or Crown Chakra (purple)

This chakra is located just behind the top of the skull. It is the center of spirituality, enlightenment, dynamic thought and energy. It allows for the inward flow of wisdom, and brings the gift of cosmic consciousness.

When the crown chakra is blocked or out of balance, there may be a constant sense of frustration, no spark of joy, and destructive feelings. Illnesses may include migraine headaches and depression; as well as, energetic disorders; brain tumors; amnesia; and sensitivity to light, sound and other environmental factors.

Chapter 20

ACCIDENTS

Accidents are never accidents. They are just like illnesses in that they are trying to deliver messages. If you are not hearing the messages being delivered in any other way, you will find more drastic measures to get the word to yourself. It is probably an important message if you feel you must resort to these measures. Maybe you are super "hard headed" and require stronger messages than a kind "tap on the shoulder."

Look at accidents in the same way as symptoms in the body as to what the message is that is trying to be delivered. I'm just now being told to call them "message incidents" rather than "accidents." Hmmm, that's interesting – completely says it as it is. Look at the part of the body that is being affected and that will start giving you your answers.

Some of the different types of "accidents" people have are: slipping and falling, cuts and bruises, running into things, and slamming their fingers (or other body parts) in doors/windows/with hammers. I know there are probably many more you can think of, but these will suffice for now so you can see how this messaging works.

My first thought as I think about someone or myself slipping on something, is that of not feeling as though I am on solid ground. "The ground beneath me is slippery." Maybe also of not being committed to a certain course of action or direction.

Falling can be the loss of balance, or the ground or your foundation is not stable and you cannot stand on it. Maybe you are not feeling secure in your decisions. Like, "You don't have a leg to stand on." Wow – that one could work for several things! See how literal these things are? It always amazes me! Just look at what is or was going on at the time of the incident to get a better understanding of the message.

Cuts can indicate a break in your barrier. Your skin is your body's protection and now it is open. It could also represent feeling vulnerable.

Running into things might be telling you to slow down and pay attention to where you are going; to details; to life in general. "They" say repeatedly to "stop and smell the roses – bring more joy into your lives." This might be another such message.

Slamming and smashing body parts really feels like their trying very hard to get your attention. As in some of the messages, "they" want you to stop and listen. Maybe this is one of those types of messages. It might also be to slow down and pay attention as with the running into things.

Many of our "message incidents" happen while we are in our automobiles. If you think about it, our car is our vehicle to get us from point A to point B. That is no different than what our body is doing for our soul. So no wonder we have messages being delivered in this fashion as well.

Being "rear ended" in your car is probably a message to "get moving." "You're stuck and not moving" – it's just trying to get you to move off of this place of indecision or non-movement. Sometimes we give ourselves so many options, we become afraid to take any of them and that is when we "get stuck." At these points, any movement is better than no movement. Once you start the energies moving (even if it is a wrong direction), you will be directed in the "right" direction since nothing can happen from a place of being "stuck." I heard a statement many years ago that has stayed with me all of this time. I don't always follow it, but I am reminded of it at this time. The statement is, "Rather than trying to make the 'right' decision, make a decision and then make it 'right.'" In other words, do something and with that movement, you will see what to do next. We only become paralyzed with indecision when we are always trying to be right before we do anything.

Being hit "broad side" or from either side is probably a message that you are off track and need to shift or move to get back on track. I find many of the messages are of this nature. I think that is what we most want to do for ourselves is keep us "on track." If you notice, this type of "accident" is not trying to stop us. It is just trying to get us to veer, indicating we're a bit off track and need to be reminded to shift.

I would consider a "head on collision" to be one of trying to "stop" us on whatever path we are on.

The severity of any of these "accidents" will tell the urgency of getting the message through. It is best to get the messages earlier than later as they will get increasingly severe until you finally "get it." We can be quite "hard headed" sometimes hence the need to have such strong messages. I'm hoping that if more people understand this communication system, we can alleviate the need for so many "messages."

We can continue on this line of thinking with regards to vehicles being an extension of us and delivering messages. Let's think about some other things that happen to our cars.

My first thought is "flat tires." What happens when your car has a flat tire? It can't move. It's "stuck." This seems to be a common message. The right and left might indicate now or past incidents just as it does with the body. A "slow leak" on the tire can indicate a loss of momentum or a sluggish movement in your direction.

A few other things that happen to cars is: not being able to see out the front due to faulty wiper blades; loss of momentum due to an oil leak; loss of "grip" on the road and slipping on the road due to bald tires; inability to stop when needed due to bad or no brakes; inability to "go" because you have run out of gas; being stopped and not able to move because the transmission "falls out." The list can go on and on, but I hope you get the idea of how closely related these are. It might help to understand what is happening in your own body if you look at the car and then compare. In this way you will be more objective which enables you to understand things more clearly with all emotion removed.

I am reminded of two different clients that came in for sessions with Dolores. Each had an "accident" and wanted to know the reason for it. The first man's arm was severed when he was in school and playing with rockets in a science project. It was found during the session that he was heavily into sports and was very good. He was so good, he was headed down the path to go into professional sports. That was not the path he had set out for himself, so the best or only way to get him onto the path of choice for him was to remove the ability to use that arm which would stop the opportunity to continue in sports.

The other man was a multi-millionaire building timeshare condominiums all over the world. He was flying to a remote island to check on another building site. His friend was piloting a small two person aircraft and coming in for the landing. Where the plane would land had a steep drop off after the runway. He noticed his friend was coming in too fast and thought he would go around for another approach, but he didn't do that. With white knuckled fists on the steering wheel, he came down and went off the side of the mountain beyond the runway. The pilot was killed and this client was paralyzed from the waist down. He was in the hospital for many months, and during that time, he was not able to run his business and lost all of his holdings. During his session, the subconscious said he was going down the path of materialism and that was not his plan. He was supposed to be working on his spirituality and he never would have if he had continued on the other path.

In another case, a man was beat up and stabbed in an alley and left to die. He dragged himself to the street where he was found and taken to a hospital. He wanted to know why that happened and in his session with Dolores the Subconscious stated that those were his best friends on the spirit side who agreed to get him back "on track" if he veered off.

These are harsh examples, but they help us to understand how YOU will step in to get YOURSELF back on track if needed. There are many things to be learned and experienced in this process so it is always an opportunity for growth. Again, it must be looked at with all emotions removed. If it is really important to get you to take a different course of action, you will likely do whatever it takes to make sure that happens. There were probably many other messages and opportunities before these events that were given, but were either ignored or not understood. I believe there are points of "no return" at which some type of action must be taken to get you back on the right path or it is a completely wasted life opportunity.

Chapter 21

The Process

Here we are. This is where I tell you the secrets of how to make all of this work. As I have referenced throughout this book, there is no *one* answer or one *way* to do any of this. I will give you what has worked for me and what I have been told, but "they" have told me so many times that the most important thing is to do this work for yourself, with yourself. This is a very personal journey. Each person is finding their own ways of delivering their messages. As I have stated, there are many similarities and constants in the symbolic language, but only you will know what your individual language means to you. This is the guidance system you set up for yourself, so it is to your best interest to figure out what YOU are trying to say to YOU.

The best way to do that is to ask. Until you are able to speak directly to your Higher Self, talk to your body to see what it is trying to tell you. It may be a basic answer, but it will be something to get you moving in the direction of understanding. The main thing is that you are looking within for your answers. Your answers ARE NOT outside of yourself. You have ALL of the answers; you just don't believe it. You need some convincing and some proof. This proof won't come until you start doing it. I have said many times that this is a process. That means it is not one thing or action that is the answer. It is an accumulation of actions and things that move you to your answers and your ultimate healing. Remember, the only objective in the body delivering the messages is to get them delivered and understood. Once that has been accomplished and acted upon, there is no longer any need to deliver the message. So whatever ache, pain, or symptom was being used to deliver the message will now be gone as there is no longer any reason or need for it.

I know this sounds simplistic and may be hard to believe, but remember the Universe is not complicated, so why would you expect anything but simple?

The process is in asking the questions. If you want to know something, you ask a question. Many times, an answer to a question may lead to another question and so on, but that is how you go down the road. The questions are very important. This is true in everything you do. The question dictates the level of information given in the answer.

At first, it is easiest and probably more tangible to talk to your body. In a previous chapter, I mentioned how much the body loves for you to pay attention to it and talk to it. It is very healthful to send your body messages of love. Acknowledging the body parts for the work they do and telling them you love them. The body responds beautifully to any messages like this. You are the voice of God and it will do whatever you ask or say. It is your very willing servant – it is here to serve you in the highest manner possible. It can only do the job it is allowed to do and in the manner it is given. It will have a harder time helping you if you are treating it in an unhealthy manner. It is your home – how much are you respecting it? It is a finely tuned machine that is made to last for a very long time and heals itself if we do not interfere. Your words are very powerful. The body is always listening and will do whatever you say. Pay attention to what you are saying. I heard someone today talking about how her nose "runs all of the time." I know it never occurred to her that she is keeping that situation going because she is saying that statement. I'm sure it started innocently by her body trying to deliver a message with the sinus pressure and associated runny nose. She wasn't looking for a message (since she doesn't know about this secret message system), just a way to get the symptoms to stop, so she was taking medication. Because she didn't get to the underlying message and act on what it was trying to say, the symptoms continued. Because the symptoms continued, she is saying, "My nose is *always* running." Because she is saying, "My nose is always running," her body is listening. And being the ever vigilant servant that it is, it is saying, "Your wish is my command!" Mind your thoughts and your words! They are very powerful in that our thoughts are always creating our reality and our bodies are always listening and doing exactly as we say. Many people say, "I get a cold every winter." The body says, "Okay – I will give you a cold this winter because you told me you get a cold every winter."

It might help to look at you body as your most favorite car in the whole world. One that you saved all of your money to buy and is now your most cherished possession. You treat that differently than you do something that you do not respect. In regards to the soul traveling from body to body as it goes through lives, this may seem like a disposable body, but to this personality called "you," this is the only body you've got. This is the one you are finely tuned to and know. This is the body your soul is speaking through to you now. Please respect it and listen when it speaks.

So the first step is to get into a quiet place of mind. It can be meditation, or driving in your car with no outside noise, or taking a nice hot bath, or when you are in that quiet place just before you drop off to sleep at night. The main thing is to get to a place where there are no or low sounds and no distractions. Talk to the body part that is having issues. If it is the knee, talk to the knee. Say, "What are you trying to tell me?" "What do you want me to know?"

129

Whatever you hear (even if it doesn't make any sense) is your answer. Trust the very first thing that comes into your mind. It may come as a wee small sound. And this sound is like a whisper inside your head – it won't be a physical sound you hear outside of yourself. You may get a visual of an answer or you may get a knowing of something. In other words you may see a picture that is for you to evaluate and translate for the answer. The knowing is where you just know something. You don't know why or how you know, you just know that you know. That is fine. Our abilities to receive information come in many different forms. There is no one way that is the right way. The main thing I can tell you about this is to TRUST what you hear (or see, or know, etc.).

So the first step is to ask and receive and trust the answer. The previous chapters on the body parts and the messages they mean will help give guidance as to what it may be trying to tell you. It is all right if you do not receive an answer right away. This is the beginning of the process and your body is not used to you speaking to it, so be patient. Your soul will find other ways to get the answer through to you as well. It may come from someone saying something to you, or a book falls open to a certain page, or the radio or television may have some information. The main thing you are trying to accomplish at this point is to go inward and listen.

Once you have received an answer, or even if you haven't quite got all of it, you can now have a conversation with this part. Let's say it is your knee and your message is that you are being indecisive about moving in a new direction. Once you understand that as the message for you, you can talk to the knee and thank it for doing its job in such a beautiful manner and that now you understand and will make a decision and commit to the direction decided upon. This step could be termed "message delivered and understood."

Next, you must take action. It is one thing to say you understand and have made a decision. It is quite another to actually take the steps in the new committed direction. This is the action step. You must take the action or it is not seen that the message has been delivered.

I feel the need to acknowledge that this is a planet of free will and you do not have to do whatever it is that your soul wants you to do. But please remember that your soul is the one with the overview and can see the big picture of what you came to learn and do. This is the communication system you set up to help yourself in this maze called life. You can choose to not listen and do it your way, but understand you will have a body that is out of sync and may have major health issues and symptoms, since this is one of its major roles and agreements it took on when it became your body. I don't think you would be reading this book if that is your state of mind, so I'm not sure why "they" had me put that in. I do not proclaim to know all of the answers. Ask your own questions to find the meanings for yourself.

Once you are solidly on your new path of direction, your symptoms will disappear. When you no longer need to receive the message, the message will disappear.

Sometimes the message is coming from an event from another life. There are some similarities or some reason it is showing it to you now. You must use some investigative, detective skills sometimes, but that is part of the process as well. It may be very beneficial to have a QHHT session from one of the many trained practitioners. The key is to get to the source of the situation. Once you do, the rest will fall into place as it is very difficult to go back or unlearn something once you have taken that step.

I will reiterate the steps now:

1. Ask your body or Higher Self what it is trying to tell you.
2. Listen for the answer.
3. Acknowledge and be thankful for the answer.
4. Take action on the information received.
5. Enjoy your new course of action in your symptom free life!

As I said previously, the steps are simple and easy, but sometimes when something is seen as so simple, it is devalued. This absolutely works if you will do it. As you get comfortable with talking to your body, you will see that the communication can and will continue in other ways and you will soon find that you are talking directly with your Higher Self. At some point it is easy to carry on a conversation. It is all a matter of trusting what you are receiving. It is always positive as this part always has your highest good at heart. Anything that you may receive that is not of the highest is your fear. Please refer back to the chapter on fear to fully understand how this energy manifests. It is all of your own making and you never have anything to be afraid of. It is all and always for your highest good.

Chapter 22

Body Messages – Quick Reference Guide

Following is a list of very common ailments and very brief descriptions of possible messages. It is highly encouraged that you read the sections that fully explain why the different body parts have the messages that they do rather than just take my information here. As I have said before, I do not proclaim to have all of the answers. You need to ask your own questions to get the information that is correct for you. Some of these messages came from hypnosis sessions and many came from me intuitively "feeling" my way into the illness or disease process to see what they had to "say."

Abdominal Cramps: Holding in of emotions and thoughts; not releasing emotions.

Abscess: Anger not expressed. (The location of the abscess will give more insight about the anger)

Accidents: Messages (The type of accident will give more insight as to the message.)

Aches: An attempt to get your attention. (The location of the ache will give more insight about the message)

Acne: Trying to hide. Not feeling "good enough." Little bits of anger coming to the surface.

Addictions: A need to control your surroundings.

Adenoids: Not able to express yourself or say what you want.

AIDS: Feeling shame; extreme guilt. Fear of judgment.

Alcoholism: Desire to escape and not be present.

Allergies: Many allergies are from past-life traumas.

Alzheimer's Disease: Desire to leave the body, but very gradually to help those around them accept.

Amnesia: Denial of present situation; escape.

Anemia: Not recognizing one's self value; a feeling of weakness.

Ankle Problem: Not being flexible in moving in a new direction.

Anorexia: Wanting to disappear; not wanting to be here.

Anus Problems: Not wanting to "let go" of issues; a desire to control situations and people.

Anxiety: Not trusting the Universe/Higher Self/anything outside of self.

Apathy: Not engaged in the flow or joy of life.

Appendicitis: Anger at one's inability to release emotions.

Arm Problems: Issues with accepting and embracing love and affection.

Arteriosclerosis: The joy is missing in your life. Becoming hardened to life.

Arteries: The flow of life. Joy.

Arthritis: Being inflexible in movement and attitudes towards a new direction in life. In hands: trying to hold onto something or someone.

Asthma: Feeling constricted in life; not able to move freely; can also be from past-life death

Athlete's Foot: Issues with "stepping out" in new direction.

Back Problems: Carrying a heavy load and not feeling supported.

Lower/Middle Back (The support system): Not feeling supported.

<u>Upper Back, Neck & Shoulder Tension</u>: Carrying other people's problems, feeling like you have the whole world on your shoulders.

<u>Balance, Loss of</u>: Indecisive; not sure of next move.

<u>Bedwetting</u>: Not feeling secure in release of emotions.

<u>Birth Defects</u>: Karmic; you decide and plan entire blueprint of the body before coming in.

<u>Bladder Problems</u>: Issues with releasing something. (Fear of keeping it or of letting it go.)

<u>Bleeding</u>: Feeling out of control with your own life force.

<u>Bleeding Gums</u>: Feeling out of control of what you are saying.

<u>Blood</u>: Life force of the body.

<u>Blood Problems</u>: Issues with how you see your life. Lack of joy and "life" to your life.

<u>Blood Pressure</u>: Lack of trust in the world around you.

<u>Body Odor</u>: Self-dislike; attempting to repel others' attention.

<u>Bones</u>: Framework of the body.

<u>Bone Problems</u>: Issues with your plans; not feeling secure with decisions.

<u>Bowels</u>: Waste elimination of the body.

<u>Bowel Problems</u>: Issues with eliminating the waste in your life. Fear of letting go.

<u>Brain</u>: Central computer or message "sender and receiver" of the body.

Brain Problems: Issues with receiving messages; resistance to input of information.

Breasts: Nurturing center of the body.

Breast Problems: Issues/anger with nurturing; not being nurtured or not able to nurture.

Breathing Problems: Not partaking in life. Afraid of life.

Bronchitis: Shutting down of the life force. Constriction of desires.

Bruises: Not paying attention to self.

Burns: An urgent message to pay attention. (The location of the burn will give more insight as to the message.)

Cancer: Severe hate and/or resentment/anger toward another individual, but not expressing it openly; anger turned inward.

Canker Sores: Angry words wishing to be expressed.

Cataracts: Not wanting to see what's ahead; fear of the future.

Chills: A desire to withdraw from social situation.

Chronic Diseases: Resistance to understand the messages.

Colds: Indecisiveness, need to make decision and not doing so; feeling sorry for self and wishing to delay activity. Are over worked and needing to rest.

Colitis and Elimination Problems: Over attachment, not releasing situations.

Coma: Total escape from a situation.

Conjunctivitis: Angry at what you are seeing. Not wanting to face a situation.

Constipation: What are you trying to hold onto?

Cysts: Anger. The location will give more insight as to what you are angry about.

Cystic Fibrosis: Not feeling free to live your life; feeling constricted.

Deafness: Refusal to listen. What don't you want to hear?

Depression: Escape from the present.

Diabetes: Lack of sweetness/love in your life.

Diarrhea/Frequent Urination: What are you trying to move quickly from your life?

Digestive Disorders: What's going on that you're not able to "stomach"?

Dizziness: Not feeling centered. Feeling unstable or indecisive.

Ears: Sensory organ for hearing.

Ear Problems: Issues with hearing guidance from others or ourselves.

Eczema: Too much energy coming into the body; burned in another life.

Edema: Holding on to emotions. Not allowing emotions to flow.

Elbow: The joint that allows the arms to embrace love and affection.

Emphysema: Fear of life. Afraid to "live."

Epilepsy: Too much energy coming into the body.

Eyes: Sensory organ for seeing; how we see the world around us.

Eye Disorders: Inability or refusal to see things as they really are or not wanting to look at something; not able to see the whole picture.

Farsightedness: Fear of the present.

Nearsightedness: Fear of the future.

Cataracts: Fear of seeing the situation as it is.

Glaucoma: Denial of situation

Face: How you present yourself to the world and others.

Falling Accident: Feeling insecure; not having "a leg to stand on."

Fat: Need to protect self from unwanted attention.

Fatigue: Attempt to escape from present situation.

Feet: Move you into new directions and situations.

Feet Problems: Resistance to moving in new direction.

Female Problems: Not feeling creative. Feeling victimized. Having issues with your femininity.

Fibroid Tumors: Feeling guilt or grief for lost pregnancies; great desire to have children.

Foot, Leg or Hip Pain: Not going in the right direction, or holding back on what they should be doing.

Gallstones: Rigidity or hardening of thought processes.

Gangrene: A desire to leave this life "one piece at a time."

Gas Pains: Difficulty digesting thoughts or emotions.

Gastritis: Inability or unwillingness to release angry emotions.

Hands: Hands are used to accept and hold things; also used for tools.

Headaches: Pressure/stress in this life or possibly from past-life trauma.

Hearing Disorders: Inability or refusal to listen or accept what is heard. Not wanting to hear something.

Heart Attack: Feeling pressured by responsibility; wanting to escape.

Heart Problems: The heart is the seat of the emotions, problems with the love life.

<u>Hemorrhoids</u>: Need to get "off your butt" and start moving; something is a "pain in the butt."

<u>Hepatitis</u>: Angry at a toxic situation.

<u>Hernia</u>: Constriction of emotions; feeling you cannot express your emotions.

<u>Herpes</u>: Feeling shame or guilt of sexuality.

<u>Hip</u>: Joint that allows the leg to bend and move.

<u>Hip Problems</u>: Resistance in moving in desired direction.

<u>Hives</u>: An irritation from the inside out; eating yourself up with worry.

<u>Impotence</u>: Feeling the victim; issues with masculinity; overpowered by a female. Vow of celibacy in a past-life.

<u>Incontinence</u>: Feeling powerless; loss of control.

<u>Indigestion</u>: Not feeling comfortable with something you are doing or saying.

<u>Infection</u>: Anger at self. The location of the infection will give insight as to what that anger is about.

<u>Inflammation</u> – "Itis": Angry thoughts at self or something. (The location of he inflammation will give more insight of the issue.)

<u>Influenza</u>: Feeling vulnerable; a victim; needing a rest.

<u>Ingrown Toenail</u>: Resistance to move forward.

Insanity: Escape from the present reality; not taking responsibility for yourself.

Insomnia: Fear usually from a situation that happened in childhood.

Itching: Desire to move and "get going."

Jaw Problems: Not speaking your truth; fear of rejection; fear of not being "good enough."

Joints: Flexible points in the body that allows bones to move.

Kidney Disorders: What are you trying to get out of your life? What is poisoning your life?

Knees: Points of flexion of the legs; allow the legs to move.

Knee Problems: Resistance to move in your desired direction in life.

Laryngitis: Inability or fear to speak up.

Legs: Part of the body that moves you and carries you forward.

Leg Problems: Resistance to moving forward.

Leukemia: Desire to leave this life and planet.

Liver: Filters toxins from the body.

Liver Problems: Your having an issue with a toxic situation or actual toxins or poisons in your life.

Lupus: Attacking yourself; feeling a need to be punished.

Lymph Problems: Feeling you are under attack and in the victim mode.

Lung Disorders (Asthma): Feeling restricted, feeling smothered by individuals or situations.

Menopause Problems: Feeling you are losing your personal power; not feeling creative.

Menstrual Problems: Resistance to moving into your feminine power; not feeling creative.

Migraine Headaches: Residue of past-life trauma.

Mouth Problems: Not speaking your truth; need to speak out.

Multiple Sclerosis: Anger in communications; not receiving your messages.

Neck: Allows the head to move around to get different perspectives.

Neck Problems: Rigidity or lack of flexibility in seeing things from a different viewpoint or perspective.

Nervous Disorders: Stress, worry; overload of input on the system.

Nose Problems: Not willing to look at a situation that is very close to you.

Overweight: Protecting yourself from being hurt; may have starved in a past-life.

Pancreas Problems (diabetes): A lack of sweetness or joy in your life.

Paralysis: Fear or indecisiveness with your course of action. The location of the paralysis will give more insight as to the message.

Parkinson's Disease: Trying to control the people and situations around you.

Phlebitis: Blocks in the flow of the energy in your life. (The location of the clot will give more insight as to what area of your life is being affected.)

Pneumonia: Tired of life and living; loss of joy in your life.

Prostate Disorders (Male): Feeling a loss, dysfunction or misuse of power.

Rash: Irritation with a situation; the location of the rash will give more insight as to the situation.

Reproductive Disorders (Female): (Creative Center) Not appreciating the feminine expression, guilt and/or fear in expression of the receptive quality. Not feeling creative. Wanting to have children or feeling guilty for lost pregnancies.

Rheumatoid Arthritis: Holding on to something/someone very tightly. Not releasing.

Scoliosis: Not taking a stand for yourself; being wishy-washy.

Sexual Problems: Not enough or too much sex, may have taken the vow of celibacy in another life.

Sinus Problems: Pressure applied by someone close – usually yourself.

Slipping Accident: Not having a solid foundation; don't have "a leg to stand on."

Spine: The support for the body; it holds the body up.

Spinal Curvature: Not standing up for what you believe; being wishy-washy.

Stomach Problems: Holding your emotions in and not releasing them; not able to "stomach" something or "digest" some words or thoughts.

Swelling: Not releasing your emotions; the location will give more insight as to what the emotions are about.

Tape Worm: Feeling the victim; what is eating at you?

Teeth Problems: Fear or inability to speak your truth.

Thyroid Problems: Fear that what you have to say is not important.

Tinnitus: Not listening to your guidance. Can also be a calling to raise your frequency.

Throat Disorders: Not speaking your truth or holding back. Fear of speaking out.

Ulcers: What's "eating" you? Are you allowing others to control you?

Urinary Infections: You need to release a toxic situation from your life.

Uterus: The creative center and female power zone.

Venereal Disease: Feeling shame or guilt with sexuality; may have taken a vow of celibacy in another life.

Warts: Feeling ugly; feelings of self hate.

Index

Index

Index

Index

Index

Index

Julia Cannon

Julia became a registered nurse and worked in Intensive Care and Home Health for the duration of her 20+ year career. She then decided to explore other aspects of the healing profession and has trained in Reconnective Healing and Dolores Cannon's Quantum Healing Hypnosis Therapy.

Her energy healing has taken on its own dimension and has formed into something she calls "Lightcasting." Intuitive lights come from the hands to direct energy where it is needed to balance any deficiencies in the body. This balancing may be happening on the physical, mental and/or spiritual level. While she is working in someone's energy field, she gets intuitive messages/impressions of what is happening and what is needed to help the person bring about their healing.

When Julia does remote energy work, she is taken intuitively inside the body to see what the condition looks like and then she is given methods to correct the situations. This has been a spontaneous development that continues to amaze her in its applications.

Other Books By Ozark Mountain Publishing, Inc.

Dolores Cannon
Conversations with Nostradamus,
    Volume I, II, III
Jesus and the Essenes
They Walked with Jesus
Between Death and Life
A Soul Remembers Hiroshima
Keepers of the Garden.
The Legend of Starcrash
The Custodians
The Convoluted Universe - Book One,
    Two, Three, Four
Five Lives Remembered
The Three Waves of Volunteers and the
    New Earth
Stuart Wilson & Joanna Prentis
The Essenes - Children of the Light
Power of the Magdalene
Beyond Limitations
Atlantis and the New Consciousness
The Magdalene Version
O.T. Bonnett, M.D./Greg Satre
Reincarnation: The View from Eternity
What I Learned After Medical School
Why Healing Happens
M. Don Schorn
Elder Gods of Antiquity
Legacy of the Elder Gods
Gardens of the Elder Gods
Reincarnation...Stepping Stones of Life
Aron Abrahamsen
Holiday in Heaven
Out of the Archives – Earth Changes
Sherri Cortland
Windows of Opportunity
Raising Our Vibrations for the New Age
Michael Dennis
Morning Coffee with God
God's Many Mansions
Nikki Pattillo
Children of the Stars
A Spiritual Evolution
Rev. Grant H. Pealer
Worlds Beyond Death
A Funny Thing Happened on the Way to
    Heaven
Maiya & Geoff Gray-Cobb
Angels - The Guardians of Your Destiny
Seeds of the Soul
Sture Lönnerstrand
I Have Lived Before
Arun & Sunanda Gandhi
The Forgotten Woman
Claire Doyle Beland
Luck Doesn't Happen by Chance

James H. Kent
Past Life Memories As A Confederate
    Soldier
Dorothy Leon
Is Jehovah An E.T
Justine Alessi & M. E. McMillan
Rebirth of the Oracle
Donald L. Hicks
The Divinity Factor
Christine Ramos, RN
A Journey Into Being
Mary Letorney
Discover The Universe Within You
Debra Rayburn
Let's Get Natural With Herbs
Jodi Felice
The Enchanted Garden
Susan Mack & Natalia Krawetz
My Teachers Wear Fur Coats
Ronald Chapman
Seeing True
Rev. Keith Bender
The Despiritualized Church
Vara Humphreys
The Science of Knowledge
Karen Peebles
The Other Side of Suicide
Antoinette Lee Howard
Journey Through Fear
Julia Hanson
Awakening To Your Creation
Irene Lucas
Thirty Miracles in Thirty Days
Mandeep Khera
Why?
Robert Winterhalter
The Healing Christ
James Wawro
Ask Your Inner Voice
Tom Arbino
You Were Destined to be Together
Maureen McGill & Nola Davis
Live From the Other Side
Anita Holmes
TWIDDERS
Walter Pullen
Evolution of the Spirit
Cinnamon Crow
Teen Oracle
Chakra Zodiac Healing Oracle
Jack Churchward
Lifting the Veil on the Lost Continent of
    Mu
Guy Needler
The History of God
Beyond the Source – Book 1

For more information about any of the above titles, soon to be released titles,
or other items in our catalog, write or visit our website:
PO Box 754, Huntsville, AR 72740
www.ozarkmt.com

Other Books By Ozark Mountain Publishing, Inc.

For more information about any of the above titles, soon to be released titles,
or other items in our catalog, write or visit our website:
PO Box 754, Huntsville, AR 72740
www.ozarkmt.com